IDEAS OPINION *The* EXPLANA— CONVENTIONS *Writing* ARGUMENT *Thief* SENTENCE FLUENCY WORD CHOICE ORGANIZATION TRAITS MODES INFORMATIONAL

Using Mentor Texts to Teach the Craft of Writing

RUTH CULHAM

INTERNATIONAL
Reading Association
800 BARKSDALE ROAD, PO BOX 8139
NEWARK, DE 19714-8139, USA
www.reading.org

The International Reading Association attempts, through its publications, to provide a forum for a wide spectrum of opinions on reading. This policy permits divergent viewpoints without implying the endorsement of the Association.

Executive Editor, Publications   Shannon Fortner
Acquisitions Manager   Tori Mello Bachman
Managing Editors   Susanne Viscarra and Christina M. Lambert
Editorial Associate   Wendy Logan
Creative Services/Production Manager   Anette Schuetz
Design and Composition Associate   Lisa Kochel

Cover   Beth C. Ford, Glib Communications and Design

Library of Congress Cataloging-in-Publication Data
Culham, Ruth.
    The writing thief : using mentor texts to teach the craft of writing / Ruth Culham.
        pages   cm
    Includes bibliographical references and index.
    ISBN 978-0-87207-099-8 (alk. paper)
    1. Language arts.   2. Children's literature—Study and teaching—Activity programs.
3. English language—Composition and exercises—Study and teaching.   I. Title.
    LB1576.C8469   2014
    372.62'3—dc23

                                        2014009325

Suggested APA Reference
Culham, R. (2014). *The writing thief: Using mentor texts to teach the craft of writing*. Newark, DE: International Reading Association.

For Sam, always

CONTENTS

ABOUT THE AUTHOR

 **Ruth Culham, EdD,** is the president of The Culham Writing Company and the former unit manager of the assessment program at Education Northwest in Portland, Oregon, USA. She was the English Teacher of the Year in Montana, the highlight of her 19-year teaching career. She holds specialty degrees in library science and elementary, middle, and secondary English education.

As a pioneering researcher in writing assessment and instruction, Ruth creates and conducts teacher workshops to provide professional development at the local, district, and state levels. At state and national conferences, she's a featured speaker on using the traits of writing, designing effective writing instruction, using reading to teach writing, and other related topics.

Ruth is the recognized expert in the traits of writing field and the author of more than 40 teaching resources published by Scholastic, including *6 + 1 Traits of Writing: The Complete Guide, Grades 3 and Up* (2003); *6 + 1 Traits of Writing: The Complete Guide for the Primary Grades* (2005); and *Traits of Writing: The Complete Guide for Middle School* (2010), the winner of a 2011 Teachers' Choice Award. (This isn't surprising since middle school is her true love.) As the author of *Traits Writing: The Complete K–8 Writing Program* (2012), she has launched a writing revolution. The program is the culmination of 40 years of educational experience, research, practice, and passion. She also wrote a new book for principals, *What Principals Need to Know About Teaching and Learning Writing* (Solution Tree, 2014).

Ruth lives in Portland, Oregon, USA, and can be reached at ruth@culhamwriting.com.

ACKNOWLEDGMENTS

*A*cknowledgments remind me of the speeches that actors give at the Oscars: I don't actually know them or their people, but I'm glad to hear that they have strong support in their professional and personal lives. I hope these acknowledgments give you a similar glimpse into my writing life and the people who made a difference in getting this book into your hands.

Let's begin with Tori Bachman, the acquisitions and development editor for the International Reading Association. Tori is smart, funny, wise, perceptive, and a great motivator. Writers need all that and more to go from an idea to a book. She found the title, *The Writing Thief*, in the Prologue and urged me to use it as a theme. As a result, I found myself morphing from the traits lady to a writing thief as the pages and chapters evolved. Thank you, Tori, for your vision and friendship that will certainly extend past the publication of this book. And thank you to the other talented, patient, and open-minded IRA staff who coaxed and encouraged at every turn.

Thank you to the children's book authors and friends who so graciously contributed their thoughts about how reading influences their writing: Ralph Fletcher, Lester Laminack, Toni Buzzeo, Lola Schaefer, David Harrison, Nicola Davies, and Lisa Yee. Your reflections add so much to the ideas in this book. Your books add so much to the reading and writing lives of children everywhere.

To Kate Messner who graciously wrote the Foreword—blowing me away with her thoughts about reading and writing. Kate, thank you for adding to this book in such a significant way. Your words are inspirational and deeply appreciated.

To Beth Ford for the most beautiful and perfect cover any author could dare to imagine. Your incredible design talent always makes me look good. And to Eva Hamaker, my wonderful assistant, who tracked down all the permissions for the everyday texts and takes such good care of me and The Culham Writing Company every day.

And finally, to a dear friend, Wendy Murray, who rode in during the cloudy days and turned them sunny.

FOREWORD

Whenever I visit schools to talk about writing books, kids inevitably ask what inspires me to write.

It's a question with a thousand answers.

I write because there are mountains and snowflakes and snakes with gorgeous patterns on their skin, because children are honest and funny and true, because the world is stunningly beautiful and painful, all at once. But beyond all of that, I write because of the books I read growing up.

Being a reader made me want to be a writer. I wanted to be part of that magic, spinning characters out of thin air, building escapes for myself, portals to worlds that were infinitely more interesting than the small town where I grew up.

You'd think that finding writing mentors in that sleepy town might have been a challenge, but it wasn't. I learned from the very best: Beverly Cleary and Judy Blume. Neither was aware that she was mentoring a strong-willed, "too full of energy" fourth grader, but that didn't matter. With Beezus and Ramona, Peter, and Fudge as their proxies, they taught me how to make characters funny and real and imperfect, how to write books that can make a reader laugh and cry. Their books taught me how to read like a writer and how to find mentors on my own bookshelf.

J.K. Rowling's Dumbledore may be every writer's dream mentor, but in the real world, mentoring usually happens in more casual ways. After all, a mentorship can be as simple as finding someone who's good at what you want to do—whether that's writing or mountain biking or knitting—and asking that person to talk with you about it a little and show you the ropes.

Kids are especially good at this. My middle school daughter has no qualms about recruiting mentors for herself. She likes to hula-hoop and once saw a college girl performing seemingly impossible tricks at a local festival. My daughter walked up, waited until the girl saw her, and then asked, "How are you doing that?" The young woman smiled, loaned my daughter a hula-hoop, taught her a handful of cool tricks, and told her where she could find more lessons online.

"How are you doing that?" Those are five powerful words that we shouldn't be afraid to ask. We can ask the question of people—and we can ask it of the books we read and love. When we read like writers, we learn to experiment with new genres, forms, structures, and styles. We learn to follow rules, but also to break them, to branch out and be brave with our words.

As lifelong readers and writers, we know this to be true. And as teachers, we must recognize that our very best resources for writing instruction aren't found in test prep programs or worksheets; they're in the books that we love as readers—the beloved stories we read growing up and the brand new titles that we can't wait to share with young readers today. Voice and word choice are traits learned through the reading of masters, and sentence structure is a skill better taught by J.K. Rowling or Katherine Paterson than some workbook writer at a testing company. Children and adults alike learn to write through reading.

Ruth's new book, *The Writing Thief*, embraces that idea. Through specific examples, it coaches educators in how to work with the very best in children's literature and beyond to teach our students how to steal—how to borrow structures and styles, how to craft beautiful phrases, and how to move readers of their own.

At the end of the day, a mentor is more than an instructor. Dumbledore doesn't just teach spells and share lemon drops; he leads by example, challenges, and lights a fire. Reading great mentor texts can provide that same inspiration for students, long after they leave the classroom. They will not only read but also write throughout their lives. They'll write because they see beauty in the world, because they are fighting for change, because they are angry or sad or joyful.

But mostly, they will write because they are readers.

Kate Messner
www.katemessner.com

PROLOGUE

I watched the movie *Kinky Boots* the other night. I enjoyed it so much that I watched it again the next night, only this time I found myself thinking about what was going on in the movie and how it was crafted. I began "reading" the movie as a writer. The first time I was totally captivated by the story line, but the second time I noticed the way the film developed, the voice of each segment, the use of language to make the theme work, and how artfully the whole piece was seamed together to create a memorable experience for the viewer. If you haven't seen this 2005 film, I highly recommend it.

The opening scene will break your heart. Much like the beginning of a great book, it grabs your attention by connecting with universal human experiences. To be sure, few of us have dealt with the stinging rebuke of a father who refuses to love a son who dresses as a woman. But who among us has not disappointed a parent and been crushed by his or her criticism? At the moment when Simon's father raps his knuckles against the window and the tone changes from young Simon's pure, unadulterated, "red high heels dancing on the boardwalk" joy to fear, then resignation, and finally despair, I remembered a time when I was rebuked by my father for something that I took pleasure in as well: creating the ultimate mudslide with the hose and a handy dirt pile. After seeing the mess that I had made, he marched me into the house to clean up and scolded me: "Girls don't play in the mud like this. Shame on you." I was wounded to the quick, and the memory still haunts me. Voice is the trait of writing that reaches out to readers and draws them in. This moment of voice in *Kinky Boots* resonated deeply within my long-ago child self.

As the story unfolds (spoiler alert!), we meet another set of father and son characters, the Prices. During a poignant scene, the son, Charlie, receives a phone call. He never says that his father died, but you just know it, and sure enough, the next scene is at the funeral. We get this key information through gesture, tone, and of course, the look on Charlie's face. We don't need to be told that something terrible happened that will change Charlie's life because we've been shown it.

Later in the film, there's a pleasant sense of completeness when the scene on the boardwalk is reprised. The dancing image is called back, this time with Simon dressed as Lola, the adult, trying to recapture the magic of those childhood moments when the need to dance in high heels outweighed any punishment that the father could threaten. It serves to deepen a character element of the film and position the viewer/reader for the bigger ending. The scene is perfectly placed in the organization of the narrative, the same as a writer tries to do with key pieces of information or story elements in text. Having good ideas is critical, but as any reader will tell you, they have to be revealed logically so the entirety of the story line adds up to something important by the end.

When I finished watching *Kinky Boots* the second time, I was ready to watch it again because I wanted to look even closer at how masterfully the different ideas fit together.

This leap from watching the movie to experiencing it as a writer reminded me of what an exciting challenge it is to find the right texts, the right moments, and the right images to show students how different elements of writing work. I am always on the hunt for mentor texts, and because I'm a reader and a writer, I find great stuff. I look at the world of print and nonprint through the eyes of a writing thief because I search for models of good writing that can inspire students to look at writing from a fresh perspective, try new writing techniques, and turn ordinary writing into something extraordinary.

> 66 I am always on the hunt for mentor texts, and because I'm a reader and a writer, I find great stuff. 99

Recently, I picked up the "do not disturb" signs from a Sheraton hotel. I was leaving early from Raleigh, North Carolina, for the trip home to Portland, Oregon, and I noticed that the door hangers were new, fun, and eye-catching: "I need some 'me time.' Please do not disturb," "I need a moment. Make that thirty moments. Please do not disturb," and, "I'm good to go. Please do not disturb." It made me wonder why a big hotel chain would go to the expense and trouble to revise an already clear, succinct direction, "Do not disturb." Their new versions added voice, a specific focus, and some fun word choice. The answer, of course, is that good writing is good business: At every level, even in this simple door hanger, it matters that the message is not only clear but also memorable.

I stole the door hangers (sorry, fellow travelers!) and will share them with students. We'll use them to try our hand at revising other familiar, everyday text messages: exit, occupied, and men/women. And we'll discuss the advantages and disadvantages of changing the message, trying new words, and adding voice to signs, which will deepen students' understanding of how important it is to communicate clearly in writing.

How did I figure out that reading informs writing? Well, there's a wealth of educational research to back up this thinking, which you'll find in Chapter 2. But mostly, experience has taught me that reading makes better writers. When I read poetry, I'm likely to try my hand at a poem or two. And while they may not be as memorable as those I've just enjoyed, writing my own provides me with a mental workout and a valuable learning experience. When I read a powerful nonfiction article, it makes me want to read more about that topic and find a way to weave that information into something I'm writing. When I see a campaign slogan, I think about how the candidate is saying a lot with a little. When I hear a song lyric that speaks to me, I find myself singing along, noticing the rhythm of the piece, and trying to replicate it in prose. I hear a powerful verb or phrase and steal it for my own writing. I'm a writing thief. It seems like every writer should be.

My experience as a reader began very young. I was read to—something I took for granted at the time but have since learned set me on the path for a lifetime of reading and writing. I learned to read because my parents smoked—true story! When I was little, it was pretty much a nightly routine that we would join my grandparents for dinner, and afterward the four adults would smoke up a storm while they talked for hours. Even then I hated smoking and couldn't wait to be excused and make my escape. The timing of my exit was critical: At a precise moment between the first and second cigarette, I would gather my plate, glass, and silverware and ask to be excused. If I asked too soon, the answer would be no. If I waited too long, I'd have to suffer another round of smoking.

I always retreated to the bathroom. My grandmother hid a stack of comic books for me under her bathroom sink—hidden because she knew my mother wouldn't approve, making them all that much more attractive to me. I remember the cartoon characters well: Huey, Dewey, and Louie;

Archie and Veronica; Atomic Mouse. My grandmother knew I'd be bored in no time on my own, and because I was the only child in the house and there was no television, she provided the wonderful contraband. I loved my grandmother for lots of reasons, but this one was high on the list.

This happened when I was only 3 or 4, at the most. I couldn't read, so all I could do was look at the pictures and try to figure out what was going on. But something magical happened during those long evenings locked away in my grandmother's bathroom. The words started to make sense. At the same time, I began writing, learning my letters from the comic books I read. I began with my name and moved on to copying words, all of this done quietly on my own in what might be the first reading/writing center in the world: my grandparents' bathroom. It was just me and comic books, paper, pencils, and crayons—plenty of resources for a motivated child to learn to read and write.

By the time I reached first grade, I was reading. Maybe not fluently or deeply, but I was reading. And because my teachers didn't know about differentiation, they stuck me in a corner of the classroom with books and left me alone. The gap between me and my peers widened, and by the end of first grade, I could read almost anything. My reading initiation may be the only good thing to come from smoking cigarettes, but I thank my grandmother for starting me on my way to a lifelong love of language.

This example repeats itself today in the literacy stories of children I know. Meet Joey Coutu, the brilliant 12-year-old son of my friend, Ray Coutu. When Joey was about 5, he was totally obsessed with Dav Pilkey's Captain Underpants series and Jeff Kinney's Diary of a Wimpy Kid series. He'd have his dad read them to him over and over and over, always delighting in the stories and how they developed in the graphic comic format. Joey began to draw and then write his own graphic novels inspired by Pilkey and Kinney. Figure 1 is an example from fifth grade of his unique way of sharing information using a format he's been playing with for years: cartoon/graphic novel.

What I notice in Joey's work is how he imitates the mentor texts that he's read in his use of the cartoon/graphic novel format, the irony in the title, the way he edited the text and added in a key missing word, and how the piece ends on the same ironic note as it begins. He chose to inform readers about Native Americans in this format because he loved the cartoons and graphic novels that he had read and studied, so he lifts the

Figure 1. Joey's Cartoon "The Native Americans"

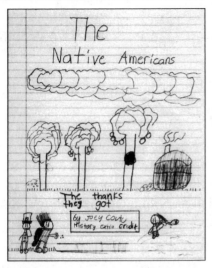

style and applies it to social studies. I love this double-dipping approach to literacy. We can use whatever catches our eye as a mentor text. As a writer myself, I use these models to dig below the surface to notice the moves the writer makes so I can try them in my own work. By stealing ideas and crafting lessons from mentor texts, I grow as a writer and learn firsthand that risk taking is one of the most significant skills that any writer can develop. I read, I write, I view, I write—it's a cycle that I have come to appreciate as a critical part of literacy.

This is close reading—where reading and writing intersect. I'm reading purposefully and uncovering layers of meaning that lead to deep analysis of the text that informs both my reading and my writing. The mentor texts that I've come to value are more than books and magazine articles. As I've indicated, they can be movies and television shows, too. They can be peanut butter jar labels and tweets. If it communicates a message clearly, it can be a mentor text.

What Lies Ahead for Prospective Writing Thieves

T.S. Eliot has been attributed as saying, "Mediocre writers borrow. Great writers steal." This book will show you how to help each of your students become a writing thief. Along with foundational understanding about teaching writing and why using mentor texts is such a powerful teaching strategy, I provide you with more than 90 examples of picture books, chapter books, and everyday texts in each of the writing modes—informational, narrative, and argument (opinion)—that can be used to show students exactly what to try in their own writing to make it stronger. Each is marked with its own icon so you can navigate through the list easily. Additionally, reproducibles and URLs for the original sources of the everyday texts are provided in the Appendix and Reference sections. You can steal the goods from me as I share all of my writing thief moves in the chapters to come.

You'll also find personal reflections from awesome children's authors that provide insight about how reading influences them as writers. I asked fiction and nonfiction authors whom I'm fortunate enough to know and call friends to share their thoughts on the subject of mentor texts.

My questions to them were, "How does reading influence your writing? Which authors have you stolen from to develop as a writer? What did you learn from these authors?" Their responses were varied and fascinating, and I hope these Author Insights sections throughout the book will give you and your students a firsthand glimpse at the power of mentor texts.

Years ago, I read that Marcel Proust wrote, "The real voyage of discovery consists not in seeking new landscapes but in having new eyes." I've never forgotten that idea. Every book, sign, menu, brochure, website, and advertisement, along with hundreds of other formats, has the potential to serve as a mentor text. You just have to see it that way. I see the world differently from most people; I see reading through the eyes of the writing thief. And because you're reading this book, you might be thinking about reading like a writing thief, too.

AUTHOR INSIGHTS: *Lester Laminack*

 It may seem odd, but as a child, I was not an avid reader. I was able, just not avid. I certainly loved a good story, and I relished those times when some adult would lean in and commence with, "Did I ever tell y'all about that time when…?" Although I didn't fall quickly into books, reading became more important to me as I grew older. Stories were, and continue to be, my preference. Even so, I spent my share of time stretched out on the floor, propped up on a sofa cushion, pilfering through pages of some volume or another of Compton's Encyclopedia, soaking up facts about a foreign land, a famous person, or an exotic animal.

Today, as an avid reader, I consume a great variety of texts, including picture books of all types, young adult literature, newspapers, magazines and journals, biographies and memoirs, and both fiction and nonfiction for adults, and I have a strong affection for poetry. But I'm most drawn to the voices of Southern writers such as Flannery O'Connor, Eudora Welty, Reynolds Price, Carson McCullers, Clyde Edgerton, Lee Smith, Kaye Gibbons, Mark Childress, Jill McCorkle, Tommy Hays, and Ron Rash, to name a few. I'm fairly certain that being bathed in story, splashing about in the warm Southern voices of my people, is what attuned my ears to the music of language and sends me, even now, in search of Southern writers. When I read them, I hear my people speak, and see my landscapes unfold. I live there among them in those pages. I am certain that my insights about voice have roots in my reading each of their voices and recognizing my own among them.

Of course, I read outside the boundaries of Southern fiction, and when I do, I prefer books about folks making the most of ordinary life. From reading, I have learned to value the most mundane details of everyday life. I have come to recognize that ordinary life is a catalog of conflicts and tensions, characters, and plots essential to writing.

As one who writes for children, I am informed and inspired by many, but there are a handful of children's authors whose writing I keep close at hand: Ezra Jack Keats, Mem Fox, Patricia MacLachlan, Cynthia Rylant, and Jacqueline Woodson. Each of these writers masterfully manages aspects of their craft in ways I aspire to. So, when I hit a wall (or more likely dig a hole I can't get out of), I step away from my writing to consume theirs.

Keats creates story in such tidy packages with near perfect balance. His language is accessible without being oversimplified. His topics zero in on an aspect of childhood shared by children everywhere. Fox has rhythm; there is such music on her pages, and I know of no one who can pack such power in so few words. MacLachlan has the most beautiful cadence in her writing. The prose is poetic and rich without being heavy or dense. I savor her language as I do a fine truffle and an exquisite glass of cabernet. Rylant brings voice to the surface and lifts the importance of place (as does George Ella Lyon, by the way). And Woodson, well she just amazes me by her ability to take on tough and often sensitive topics with elegance, grace, and truth. I want to write like these folks. We all need someone to look up to.

So, when I sit down to write, I am never alone. Every writer I have ever read is somewhere in the room reading my words as they appear on the screen, listening in as I read my own words aloud to myself, whispering to me, coaching my next move.

And now, may you find what you need to turn yourself into a world-class writing thief with every page that follows.

CHAPTER 1

Time to Rethink
the Teaching of Writing

Writing has finally taken a place at the big family table with reading and math. It's long overdue. There is a loud clamor from educators for help with improving student writing at every age and in every subject. With this elevation of standing comes pressure to succeed, and succeed we must because, quite frankly, we're not doing a credible job of teaching writing in U.S. schools. In October 2012, the National Center for Education Statistics published its results of the 2011 National Assessment of Educational Progress (NAEP) for writing in grades 8 and 12. The results were dismal. Only 27% of the nation's eighth graders perform at or above the proficient level. Only 27%. And of that group, only 3% were advanced. That means 73% of eighth graders couldn't write at the proficient level. And the results for grade 12 were worse because the numbers were the same, 27% proficient and 3% advanced, meaning that in four years there were no measurable gains. This is abysmal, and I'm sure you're shaking your head right along with me at these numbers.

The U.S. Department of Education (2012) also published these results: Student writing was 8 points down on the SAT since the inception of the direct writing assessment from an average score of 497 in 2006 to 489 in 2011. These numbers are in line with the findings from Graham and Perin (2007) that 70% of students in grades 4–12 are considered low-achieving writers. Graham and Perin argue the following for the 21st century:

> Writing well is not just an option for young people—it is a necessity. Along with reading comprehension, writing skill is a predictor of academic success and a basic requirement for participation in civic life and in the global economy. (p. 3)

But from all available information, we seem to have a long way to go to make writing well a reality for today's students.

The news about reading and literacy in general isn't any better. According to a study conducted in late April 2013 by the National Institute of Literacy (U.S. Department of Education, 2013), 14% of the population (32 million adults) in the United States can't read, 21% of adults read below the fifth-grade level, and 19% of high school graduates can't read. Unfortunately, even though reading and literacy have been on the educational radar for years, this literacy rate isn't any better than it was 10 years ago when the National Assessment of Adult Literacy (U.S. Department of Education, n.d.) reported that 14% of adults in the United States in 2003 demonstrated a below-basic literacy level, and 29% percent exhibited a basic reading level.

There are many reasons the United States isn't making progress toward critical literacy goals, including the quality of education and the poverty rate in this country, which undermine the conditions needed for students to learn. Measures of socioeconomic status—a combination of education, income, and occupation—spotlight the literacy gap between the haves and the have-nots. Muijs (2010), in his work on socioeconomic status and its impact on education, points out that reaching more students to make gains in literacy rates will be a challenge because it requires skilled and highly qualified teachers. He notes that our most successful teachers are rarely found in the schools and classrooms of children from the least privileged communities, thus assuring the literacy gap for generations to come.

Stephen Krashen's (2011a, 2011b) research and understanding about the effects of poverty also shed light on literacy rates. Drawing from his own work and the work of other key educational researchers on poverty and its effect on learning, he concludes that 20% of U.S. children come from high-poverty families, the highest level of any industrialized country, and have very little access to books at home, at school, and in their communities. Krashen notes that when children have access to reading material, they read. And what is of particular interest to note is that reading has been shown to improve "all aspects of [children's] literacy, including vocabulary, grammar, spelling, reading and writing ability" (2011, para. 8).

As we've known for many years, the crisis in public education can be remedied by these two factors: students' access to great texts, and great teaching. We must close the education gap by leveling the playing field for all students. This does not mean more tests, by the way. Our rallying cry should be, "Texts not tests." Every student deserves a highly qualified writing and reading teacher and a wealth of reading and writing resources—no matter where they live: urban or rural; the North, South, East, or West.

Many schools I visit have been thinking about and implementing new educational systems and ways of thinking about teaching and learning for a number of years. They've been grappling with issues of poverty and how it affects the students in their schools, right along with delivering professional development to create teachers who are highly skilled and able to deliver the goods for students in all socioeconomic groups.

> **"** Our rallying cry should be, "Texts not tests." **"**

Recently, I was in Illinois working with a very forward-thinking and dedicated group of teachers. After a discussion about how writing instruction was going in their schools, one teacher raised her hand and asked me probably the most important and insightful question that anyone has ever asked in my 25 years of conducting professional development across the country and around the world. Her eyes locked with mine as she probed, "*Why* aren't we doing better? So many of us are teaching writing the best way we know how. Why isn't it paying off?"

Bingo. This is the jackpot question, the mother of all issues in the writing instruction world. Why aren't students writing better? I took a deep breath and thought for a moment. Such a smart question deserved an equally smart answer, so I turned it back to the group to discuss for a few minutes, and then we shared our conclusions. Interestingly, each group of teachers came up with the same point: consistency. There is little or no continuity in the teaching of writing. Most schools don't have a scope and sequence or a set of materials and strategies that outlines a core writing curriculum for each grade and across grades. So, although students may have an exemplary writing experience and make great gains one year, they start all over the next year because the new teacher doesn't know what was taught the previous year or has a different set of objectives in mind. Think of the impact on student writing performance when this happens year after year after year.

Several of the teachers in Illinois said they had participated in curriculum-mapping activities to track writing lessons and develop a scope and sequence of writing skills taught each year. They were shocked to discover that many of the same lessons taught in fourth grade, for instance, were also taught in eighth grade. There was no evidence of scaling up with skills instruction over time. A lesson on sentence beginnings in second grade, for instance, looked exactly like a lesson in fifth grade on that same topic. "No wonder students aren't improving," one teacher noted. "We're not challenging them or deepening their learning by approaching our teaching systematically and with increasing complexity over time. If anything, we're leading them to slow writing deaths."

There are actions that we can take to make sure students are in classrooms where writing contributes to overall academic success. We can develop curriculum that is based on essential writing skills and make sure it deepens over time, becoming more complex and more integrated every week, month, and year. We can examine current teaching practices for effectiveness and discard old ways of doing things that simply don't work. We can reinforce for students that writing well is a goal worth shooting for every single day.

To accomplish this, we should teach children that writing is thinking and, as such, that it's never easy, always messy, yet ultimately satisfying to get right. It's satisfying because the writing they do matters to them. Students should always know and embrace the relevance of what they compose from the onset. This is how we get buy-in for writing. Whether a sentence, a paragraph, or a page, the child engaged in the tough but transformational work of writing is egged on by the motivation to reach his or her audience in some purposeful way. That purpose could be as concrete as a movie or book review or as atmospheric as how the teacher makes it clear that writing is thinking, but it's in the air of the classroom, and the students breathe it: Writing isn't just for poets; it's for life.

Here's the bottom line: It's a happy, new day for writing instruction. There's a renewed interest and emphasis on how to improve the literacy lives of children everywhere. I welcome everyone's ideas about how to create continuity in writing instruction so students move forward in a purposeful and meaningful way. It's a big table, and there is plenty of room for multiple perspectives on how to get the job done, but it needs to happen now. Too many children are counting on us to get it right—now.

Start Here: Stop Doing Dumb Things

We do a lot of sensible things in teaching, but we also do a lot of dumb things. As workshops and professional development sessions point out and from our own understandings as writing teachers, we're aware of the things that work and don't work. Yet, we keep doing many of the wrong things anyway because we don't know what else to do or just don't want to change. I call these zombie practices: We think we kill them, but they just keep coming back to life.

I propose we stop doing anything that is not a proven, documented, successful practice and focus on how to help every teacher feel comfortable with and capable of implementing the most dynamic writing practices as we learn to make wise instructional decisions for and with student writers.

So, how do you spot dumb things? For starters, when students groan, don't want to write, and have to be dragged through the writing process and into conferences, something's not right. Maybe it's the topic, maybe it's their history with writing, or maybe it sounds flat-out scary to think of putting words on a page for any number of reasons. Whatever is making your writing students sick, diagnose it and provide an antidote quickly, before the patient dies. Table 1 is a starter list of things that don't work and some alternatives that you can try instead.

Abandoning time-honored practices is not a simple thing. If you were taught (as I was) to diagram sentences over and over; write five-paragraph essays; learn grammar, spelling, and vocabulary from lists; and other traditional practices, it's likely that you're teaching using those same methods. I did. When I began teaching, I replicated how I was taught, and it didn't work. My students hated to write, and I hated to spend time teaching it. It wasn't until I went to the Montana Writing Project and learned how to write myself that I began to change my teaching. If we're honest about our collective practices, we can find many to jettison

Table 1. Dumb Things Versus Sensible Things in Writing Instruction

Dumb Things	Sensible Things
Using worksheets	Practicing new skills in writing created by the student
Giving Friday spelling tests	Developing control over spelling words by using multiple methods, such as high-frequency words, word families, phonetics, sight words, spell-check, and other resources
Assigning vocabulary lists	Exploring word meanings and developing a fascination for language
Prescribing formats, such as topic sentence plus three supporting details, and five-paragraph essays	Allowing the ideas to determine the organization, based on the purpose for the writing
Teaching skills in isolation	Teaching in the context of reading, skill by skill, always moving toward deepening understanding of text
Assigning topics every time students write	Providing choice in format, genre, and mode
Grading based on compliance and following directions	Evaluating based on performance, noting growth, and celebrating effort
Covering everything every year	Using a spiraling scope and sequence of writing skills that builds one year upon the next
Writing in absolute quiet	Creating a happy, working classroom in which students freely share, ask questions, and discuss
Dwelling on test preparation	Teaching the test format as a genre of reading and writing
Marking papers for every possible thing that could be improved or corrected	Offering small, focused suggestions for revision and editing
Teaching writing as an isolated subject that consists mostly of grammar and other conventional practices	Teaching reading and writing together as mutually supportive language processes, one leading to the next

in favor of better methods—ones that aren't harder and more time-consuming but instead teach writing in a way that makes it easier for you and a lot more successful for students, which in turn makes teaching writing successful and, dare I say, fun.

I'm a firm believer in beginning with what we know works. To do that, it's important that we agree to put every writing practice that's present in our schools today on that table and examine it for effectiveness. And by effective, I mean we *know* that students become better writers by learning this technique, using these materials, or applying this knowledge. Take the five-paragraph essay, for example, and put it squarely down on the table. This is a zombie practice for sure! I challenge you to find empirical evidence that this technique works to create good essays. In fact, there's evidence that this formulaic way of writing actually detracts from students' abilities over time. According to the Alliance for Excellent Education (2007),

> advocates of the five-paragraph essay argue that such formulas can provide useful guidance for beginning writers, offering them a crutch upon which to rely until they are ready to try other styles and formats. However, there exists no evidence to support this theory, and most experts in writing instruction now argue that this approach does more harm than good, giving students the false impression that good writing involves nothing more than following a set of rules. Rather, the expert consensus holds that the best writing instruction teaches students to become comfortable with a wide variety of styles and formats, so they can communicate effectively with many different kinds of readers in many different contexts, adapting their writing to the particular situation and audience at hand.
>
> Moreover, experts caution that the more formulaic and constrained the assignments, the more students learn to think of writing as a rote, unengaging activity. (pp. 4–5)

We need to kill this kind of mechanized, "paint by number," zombie-style organizational strategy from our teaching world and replace it with practices that actually work. That's what this whole book is about: finding more effective ways to teach students to write by using mentor texts. Instead of telling students how many paragraphs to write or how many sentences to include in each of those paragraphs, have them look at published pieces of fiction and nonfiction and draw conclusions about how writing is structured and how long paragraphs tend to be. Ask students to note if the paragraphs are longer in informational writing or narrative, or see if they can discover the role that punctuation plays in the readability of the sentences in the paragraph. Inspire students' curiosity by looking at examples. Ask students what they find and what that might mean to them as readers and as writers. This is how you develop an energized, enthusiastic group of writers who are ready to take on the writing world. This is how students' writing will improve.

The Elephant in the Room: The Common Core State Standards

It shouldn't surprise anyone that because students' reading and writing are not at high enough performance levels to satisfy teachers, students, parents, the community, and the legislature, a national effort to find a remedy has been underway for several years. The Common Core State Standards formally entered the educational arena in 2010 and are leading the way toward an integrated approach to teaching reading and writing. Some of the standards address reading and others address writing, but teachers in every subject area are encouraged to weave them together and maximize time and resources to get better results: better readers and writers—and best of all, better thinkers.

Take a look at the Reading and Writing Anchor Standards side by side in Table 2 to see the world of possibilities for developing curriculum and planning projects to encourage students to read *and* write. As students examine texts for the writing traits and their key qualities (e.g., "Creating the Lead" in the organization trait), they do close reading of multiple texts to see how writers began similar pieces. They compare and contrast the styles of fiction leads to nonfiction leads. They develop a resource list of possible types of leads: flashback, fascinating fact, shocking statistic, dialogue, provocative phrase, and so forth. They sort them into leads that work better for fiction and those they might use for nonfiction writing. But they don't draw hard and fast lines. Writing isn't like that; the minute you reduce it to a list or a rule, you've missed the point.

After thinking, reading, and discussing the leads of multiple mentor texts, students are encouraged to revise the lead in a piece of their own. Different students will apply what they've figured out in different ways.

Table 2. Reading and Writing Anchor Standards in the Common Core[a]

Reading Anchor Standards	Writing Anchor Standards
Key ideas and details: "Read closely to determine what the text says" (p. 10), analyze for the central ideas and key interactions with the text, summarize, and make logical inferences.	*Text types and purposes:* Write narrative, informational/explanatory, and opinion/argument in print and electronic formats.
Craft and structure: Interpret words and phrases for meaning, understand how passages relate, and determine how purpose and point of view are exhibited in the text.	*Production and distribution of writing:* Use the writing process (prewriting, drafting, sharing and feedback, revising, editing, and finishing or publishing) to produce clear and coherent pieces.
Integration of knowledge and ideas: Integrate and evaluate the arguments, claims, and reasoning in two or more texts on the same topic and in diverse media formats.	*Research to build and present knowledge:* Create projects that require acquisition of information from print and electronic resources, synthesis, and written interpretation of what was learned.
Range of reading and level of text complexity: Read and understand "complex literary and informational texts independently and proficiently" (p. 10).	*Range of writing:* Write short, midrange, and long-term texts for many different purposes and in a variety of formats.

[a]National Governors Association Center for Best Practices & Council of Chief State School Officers. (2010a). *Common Core State Standards for English language arts and literacy in history/social studies, science, and technical subjects.* Washington, DC: Authors.

This is exactly what we want them to do—own it. The work on leads wasn't intended to prescribe how students begin their pieces; it was meant to open the doors of possibilities and allow students to make smart decisions for their own writing.

Reading and writing can work together to meet several of the Common Core's Anchor Standards. A mentor text–inspired activity such as this one on leads hits multiple performance targets for the Common Core:

- *Reading:* Read closely, analyze, and evaluate the content of complex texts.
- *Writing:* Conduct short research with models, draw from the evidence, revise, and integrate.

Reading and writing have a natural connection that extends into and past the Common Core. After all, the first reader of every text is the actual writer. Weaving these two literacy giants into one tapestry is not only a creative and enjoyable way to teach but also immensely beneficial. Students learn more about reading and writing when we use mentor texts to explore how writing works. I delve into this in greater detail in subsequent chapters. For now, it's enough to note that the Common Core may very well have given us the perfect excuse to officially unify the teaching of reading and writing in the English language arts and in every other content area as well, something great teachers have been doing quietly and under the radar for years. We can build a strong case for why this practice works and refine teaching strategies so every student benefits as soon as possible. Then and only then do I believe we'll see the tide of U.S. literacy begin to turn and head to shore.

Don't Forget the Importance of Excellent Teachers!

"The Standards define what all students are expected to know and be able to do, not how teachers should teach" (National Governors Association Center for Best Practices & Council of Chief State School Officers [NGA Center & CCSSO], 2010a, p. 6). This statement in the Common Core document's introduction is worthy of note. Teaching and learning is, without question, the world of the professional educator. We must not abdicate this teaching responsibility to anyone or any organization.

What could be more important for us as a community of teachers and learners than to seek and implement the best possible teaching methodology in reading and writing to impact the greatest number of students? It's our most critical priority in today's schools. The Common Core may set the standards, but teachers are the ones who will roll up their sleeves and make them attainable for their students. No one but the teacher can take materials, regardless of the source, and make them work for their students. Not surprisingly, success comes down to the teacher's ability to conceptualize the performance goals in strategies and materials that connect to all students and move them forward.

An indisputable fact that should drive educational reform is that what really influences how students learn is the effectiveness of the teacher. In their groundbreaking study on the impact of teacher effectiveness on student achievement, Sanders and Rivers (1996) may have been the first to document the differences in performance levels of students who were taught by high- and low-performing teachers. Wright, Horn, and Sanders (1997) explain this well:

> The results of this study well document that the most important factor affecting student learning is the teacher. In addition, the results show wide variation in effectiveness among teachers. The immediate and clear implication of this finding is that seemingly more can be done to improve education by improving the effectiveness of teachers than by any other single factor. *Effective teachers appear to be effective with students of all achievement levels, regardless of the level of heterogeneity in their classrooms.* (p. 63)

These findings are echoed by Sanders, Wright, and Langevin (2008), 11 years later:

> Teachers are the single most important determinant of a student's schooling experience and academic outcomes. Social science studies have demonstrated not only that highly effective teachers are capable of producing nearly three times the student achievement gains of low-performing teachers, but also that a series of five above-average teachers can overcome the deficit typically reported between economically disadvantaged and higher income students. (p. 3)

Give a good teacher an empty cardboard box, and he or she will find a way to build a writing (or reading, math, science, or the arts) curriculum around it.

Thankfully, we have more resources to use than this empty box, but the bottom line is the same. No matter what you have at your fingertips, it's how you use those resources that make a difference. That means fully understanding writing instruction practices and developing new skills in areas where we don't know as much as we should about how to help students at different stages of their writing. The goal should be to become that astonishingly good teacher who makes the difference. And to get there, we have to be willing to talk and have honest conversations (which are sometimes painful) about what we are doing and not doing at every opportunity. It isn't possible to improve student writing without them. Ineffective teaching strategies have to go, and proven, effective methods must take their place.

However, take heart that we're not doing everything wrong. In fact, a lot of what we know about high-quality writing instruction is already present in schools. I see it firsthand in my work with teachers across the country. One thing the excellent teachers have in common is that they pump up good writing practices much like an action-packed Zumba class at the end of the day. They share what they're doing and encourage others to join in. Success is contagious. The best writing teachers kill the zombies—and they stay dead.

The 4Ws of Writing

I've identified four key research-based, dynamic writing practices, or the 4Ws: writing process, writing traits, writing workshop, and writing modes. These practices are the gold standard in teaching writing. When used independently, some gain is achieved. But when combined, the potential gains are limitless. Students in classrooms that embrace all four of the Ws will meet and exceed any of the Common Core Standards or state standards. They will have rich writing lives.

I refer to the 4Ws as *dynamic,* not simply as best practices, because the word implies that there is action, movement, and progress. In becoming strong writers, we're in a constant state of learning, which leads to the application of new knowledge and skills. We're on a journey here, not simply seeking a destination. And as learners ourselves, we continue to refine our instructional practices as we understand more about how children write. Remember Proust's statement: "The real voyage of discovery consists not in seeking new landscapes but in having new eyes."

We know what a dynamic writing classroom looks like thanks to the work of many educational researchers and world-class writing teachers. It's when we see through new eyes how to embrace what works for teaching and learning about writing that we understand that we don't have to completely reinvent the teaching of writing. Rather, we need to take the dynamic practices that we already know, seek deeper understandings of the strengths of each, and apply them with fidelity for every student at every age.

To do that, we need to set the literacy table with four place settings:

1. *Writing process:* How writing is generated
2. *Writing traits:* The nuts and bolts of how writing works
3. *Writing workshop:* The organizational routines of the writing classroom
4. *Writing modes:* The purposes for writing

If you put these four elements together, writing will flourish in any classroom. Seeded by the groundbreaking work in the 1980s by Graves (1983) and Murray (1985) in their respective books *Writing: Teachers and Children at Work* and *A Writer Teaches Writing*, and Calkins's (1986) *The Art of Teaching Writing*, along with the work of many other brilliant thinkers and writers in the decades since, there couldn't be a better time to revisit these foundational understandings to move us all forward to a new era in writing instruction.

Writing Process

In the 1960s and 1970s, visionary researchers such as Janet Emig and Sondra Perl concluded that writing is not a straightforward, linear process but a search for meaning (Perl, 1994; see, e.g., Faigley, 1994). This simple but profound idea changed the writing instruction world into one whose basic tenant is that writing is a process. The steps were codified a decade later by Graves, Murray, and Calkins:

- *Prewriting:* Coming up with a topic and gathering resources
- *Drafting:* Committing initial, rough ideas to paper or digital form
- *Feedback:* Getting feedback on the draft from the reader or listener
- *Revision:* Reflecting on the feedback and implementing changes for clarity, interest, and authenticity
- *Editing:* Cleaning up the writing for the conventions: spelling, capitalization, punctuation, grammar and usage, and paragraphing

• *Finishing/publishing:* Wrapping up the task that sometimes means creating a final copy to go public

These steps are recursive, meaning it's the writer's job to apply the step of the process that is needed to move the piece forward. The writer benefits from the teacher's perspective, however, on what the next step might be. It may mean a shift of direction when a reader would be lost by what is written so far. It may mean stopping and gathering more information to add to the text. It may mean learning about and applying conventions at deeper and more thoughtful levels than previously tried. It certainly means reading and rereading to choose the best words and phrases that make the topic clear. All the steps of the writing process are available to writers every time they write. Writing is thinking aloud on paper, after all, so it shouldn't be conceived in a linear fashion. Instead, as the early writing process researchers Emig and Perl wisely point out, the process should be a search for meaning, and the writer refines thinking through revision and editing.

For more about the writing process, I recommend the seminal literature in its original form: Graves (1983), Murray (1985), and Calkins (1986).

Writing Traits

The traits are the vocabulary used to describe what good prose looks like in its different forms. It's used for formative assessment—assessment that helps teachers understand what students know and what they need help to learn. The traits are simple, logical, easy to understand, and deeply rooted in writing research, writing pedagogy, and the combined wisdom of thousands of teachers. The traits have been in the writing teacher's tool kit since first conceived in 1985, almost 30 years ago now. At the writing trait's core are fundamental principles: conducting high-quality assessment that leads to focused instruction, establishing clear goals for teaching and learning the craft of writing, using a shared vocabulary to talk about writing, and weaving together revision and editing seamlessly and strategically.

The Writing Traits

Ideas: The piece's content—its central message and details that support that message

Organization: The internal structure of the piece—the thread of logic and the pattern of meaning

Voice: The tone and tenor of the piece—the personal stamp of the writer, which is achieved through a strong understanding of purpose and audience

Word choice: The vocabulary the writer uses to convey meaning and enlighten the reader

Sentence fluency: The way words and phrases flow through the piece (It is the auditory trait because we "read" for it with the ear as much as the eye.)

Conventions: The mechanical correctness of the piece (Correct use of conventions (spelling, capitalization, punctuation, paragraphing, and grammar and usage) guides the reader through the text and makes it easy to follow.)

Presentation: The physical appearance of the piece (A visually appealing text invites the reader in.)

Four key qualities, or the different essential aspects that are measurable and teachable, further define each of these traits. These key qualities are discussed in Chapter 2. I use the four key qualities of each trait as the organizational structure for Chapters 3, 4, and 5, which include mentor texts and lesson ideas as examples of how to read like a writer in each of the modes: narrative, informational/explanatory, and argument (opinion).

For more about writing traits, I recommend my own theory and practice texts: *6 + 1 Traits of Writing: The Complete Guide, Grades 3 and Up* (Culham, 2003), *6 + 1 Traits of Writing: The Complete Guide for the Primary Grades* (Culham, 2005), and *Traits of Writing: The Complete Guide for Middle School* (Culham, 2010).

Writing Workshop

Writing workshop is a structure, a series of routines, for organizing time, resources, and interaction in the classroom that encourages active, student-centered writing activities in which students (on their own or in collaboration with others and the teacher) make decisions about what will be written. The writing workshop emphasizes the social and collaborative nature of writing and is built on the writing process model. When combined with reading instruction, the writing workshop is often referred to as the literacy workshop.

The teacher's role in writing workshops is to confer, nudge, and support students as the need arises. Most writing workshops begin with a whole-group focus lesson (often called a minilesson) that teaches students about an element of the craft of writing that the teacher has noticed needs improvement in students' writing or is part of the core grade-level curriculum. For the majority of writing workshop time, the teacher circulates around the room and meets with students individually and in small groups to help them with their writing tasks as he or she monitors progress.

There is no single writing workshop model that everyone embraces equally, but most teachers agree that providing students with choice, allowing them to work at an individualized pace, tailoring feedback so it is specific and targeted, and collaborating as writers in an environment that encourages risk taking is key to creating a successful writing experience.

For more about the writing workshop, I recommend *The Writing Workshop: Working Through the Hard Parts (And They're All Hard Parts)* by Ray (2001), *Writing Workshop: The Essential Guide* by Fletcher and Portalupi (2001), and *What You Know by Heart: How to Develop Curriculum for Your Writing Workshop* by Ray (2002).

Writing Modes

The modes are the different purposes for writing. There are three traditional prose modes: narrative, expository, and persuasive. In the Common Core State Standards, the modes have taken a front row seat in the writing arena. Purpose drives the reasons students write in all subjects and is key to helping students understand "what" they are writing. The Common Core (NGA Center & CCSSO, 2010a) revised two of the familiar modes and refined and refocused the definitions:

- *Narrative:* To write "real or imagined experiences or events using effective technique, well-chosen details, and well-structured event sequences"
- *Informational/explanatory:* "To examine and convey complex ideas and information clearly and accurately through the effective selection, organization, and analysis of content"
- *Argument (opinion):* To "write arguments to support claims in an analysis of substantive topics or texts, using valid reasoning and relevant and sufficient evidence" (p. 18)

Note that the Common Core's authors retermed *expository* to *informational/explanatory.* Either term defines the same type of writing, and I've found that this label change has not caused too much confusion. However, the authors chose to zero in on one genre of persuasive writing by selecting academic arguments (opinions), making it clear that one category or genre within the persuasive mode should be the focus of instruction. By doing this, they left out writing letters to the editor, op-ed pieces, blogs, marketing copy, public-service announcements, political cartoons, and more. The Common Core's emphasis on academic writing is understandable and even welcome, but I hope teachers will include all forms of persuasive writing in the classroom and not limit students to argument (opinion), even though this purpose for writing may be the most difficult to teach and learn well. Also note that although the Common Core focuses on more formal, academic argument writing in the upper grades, it establishes opinion writing as one of three purposes for writing in grades K–5.

For more about writing modes, I recommend *On Writing Well: The Classic Guide to Writing Nonfiction* by Zinsser (2006), *Teaching Argument Writing, Grades 6–12: Supporting Claims With Relevant Evidence and Clear Reasoning* by Hillocks (2011), and *So, What's the Story? Teaching Narrative to Understand Ourselves, Others, and the World* by Fredricksen, Wilhelm, and Smith (2012). I also highly recommend King's (2002) *On Writing: A Memoir of the Craft* not only for narrative writing advice but also for all sorts of practical writing tips.

I'm not sure which comes first, the reading or the writing. Early on in my career, the reading had the strongest impact. I immersed myself in children's books—both classics and the newer titles. I passionately studied them for pacing, vocabulary, cadence, humor, voice, leads, use of figurative language, and endings. I learned so much from reading like a writer, and I still do. However, now that my writing is a bit more focused (at least I hope it is), I think that I select the children's literature that I want to read with a more defined purpose.

For instance, I write a lot of literary or narrative nonfiction. I try to read as much of that as I can from authors whom I admire, such as Steve Jenkins, Dianna Aston, Joyce Sidman, Pam Muñoz Ryan, Jeanette Winter, April Pulley Sayre, Steve Sheinkin, and Jim Murphy. While reading these books, I study how the authors focus their ideas down to interesting nuggets that will capture readers. I look at the different nonfiction or informational text structures. I love how publishing now offers a wide selection of formats and great art design. The way in which the information is presented has a lot to do with reader participation and a choice to return to the text again and again. I notice how much critical thinking is offered in today's books. Authors, illustrators, and publishers are setting the bar high for kids. We all know they're intelligent and that they're fascinated with information that they can't find in a cursory read of an encyclopedia page or from watching 30 minutes of television.

Notes From Ruth

I'm dazzled by Lola's list of authors representing a range of different types of texts and how she draws from all of them to write her own informational works. The way she describes studying texts for structure and other writing craft is exactly what I hope this book reinforces. Her belief that critical thinking is a pivotal part of learning to write well is a notion that runs through the Common Core State Standards and can't be emphasized enough in the pedagogy of teaching writing.

Educational Shift

The teaching world is shifting more right now than at any other time in my 43-year educational career. It's exhilarating and completely terrifying at the same time. In Figure 2, this fourth-grade writer says what each of us is thinking these days and needs printed on our coffee mugs.

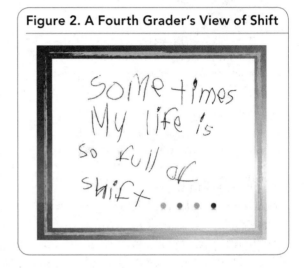

Figure 2. A Fourth Grader's View of Shift

Whether you work in a state that adopted the Common Core or not, the standards are high and the stakes are even higher that students learn to write and write well. Being an excellent teacher of writing is an activity that requires constant assessment and adjustment, based on the students and the tasks at hand. It is a dynamic practice, no doubt, and it's not easy. Writing is thinking aloud on paper, after all, and there's nothing easy about that. But it is doable. I believe that, or I wouldn't still be spending my life thinking, writing, and learning more about how to lend a hand in this critical literacy work.

Shift: It's hard. It's impossible to know where we'll end up, but one thing is for sure: We'll be further ahead in teaching writing than we are today if we keep working on improving.

When I get discouraged by results such as the 2011 NAEP report (National Center for Education Statistics, 2012), I go back to my roots as a classroom teacher—to a time and place where writing process mattered more than the prompt; where curriculum was blended in thematic units, now expanded and called project-based learning, and the flow of how the lessons and activities played out was determined by students' actions and reactions to what they were learning. Reading and writing worked together. Social studies and science were clear springboards for important questions that required research to answer and, in turn, required reading and writing skills.

I remember a time when students dived into these activities throughout the school day. I couldn't be happier that we seem to be returning to a time when we not only teach with an eye toward the Standards but also seek the joy of learning, which is infectious and lasts a lifetime. And I couldn't be happier that the rest of this book focuses on something that I've loved working on for every one of the 43 years that I've been an educator: reading and writing using mentor texts. I predict that you'll discover the joy in teaching writing when you read with a writer's eye and become a writing thief just like me.

CHAPTER 2

The Power of Mentor Texts for Writing

*L*et's be honest: We're talking about writing, and we know it's not the easiest thing to do, much less to teach. After years of studying the research and examining teachers' practices, I have found that each of the 4Ws discussed in the last chapter are big ideas on their own, but they work best fitted together, creating an instructional platform that supports the complexity of how writing is created (writing process), how it's crafted (writing traits), how the classroom operates (writing workshop), and what the different purposes are for writing (writing modes). These aren't small things to understand and teach and are likely a big part of the reason writing instruction is one of the last frontiers of educational reform for many teachers.

In this chapter, I zero in on mentor texts and the traits of writing, one of the 4Ws. In subsequent chapters, I fold mentor texts into the modes or purposes for writing: informational/explanatory, narrative, and argument (opinion).

Learning how to be a writing thief and spot the texts that show students a particular writing skill in action is an effective instructional strategy that supports deep reading, which in turn leads to deep writing. We'll get into how each of the traits help writers find what works in mentor texts as this chapter develops, but for now, let's bask in the glory of mentor texts and their role in teaching writing.

I love what Frank Smith (1994) says: "There are three parties to every transaction that written language makes possible: a writer, a reader, and a text. And of the three, the text is the pivot....[N]either writers nor readers can exist without a text" (p. 87). Texts are the glue that binds reading and writing processes together. It seems logical, then, to turn to texts to understand writing more deeply rather than relying on worksheets to figure out how writing works. By using mentor texts, the reader can virtually position him- or herself to sit beside the author and study how the text is constructed and how it communicates. It's a powerful teaching and learning strategy that we'll explore in detail in the rest of this book.

There's an abundance of educational research documenting the best instructional methods for teaching writing, including the use of mentor texts. For a good summary of those findings, look to *Writing Next: Effective Strategies to Improve Writing of Adolescents in Middle and High Schools* by Graham and Perin (2007). In this passionate call to action to improve the teaching and learning of writing, the authors cite 11 elements of effective writing instruction. Number 10 is the "study of models" (p. 5). Graham and Perin specify that "students are encouraged to analyze these examples and to emulate the critical elements, patterns, and forms embodied in the models in their own writing" (p. 20).

The Case for Mentor Texts

The term *mentor text* has a contemporary, professional cachet. I define a mentor text as any text, print or digital, that you can read with a writer's eye. I've been using this term for almost 20 years in my work with the traits and picture books. The use of models, or what I'm calling mentor texts, is a timely and practical solution for designing writing lessons in today's classrooms. In her groundbreaking text *Wondrous Words: Writers and Writing in the Elementary Classroom*, Katie Ray (1999) was one of the first to write about mentor texts as a strategy for writing. Others followed. Ralph Fletcher (2011), for example, used his own writing as mentor texts in *Mentor Author, Mentor Texts: Short Texts, Craft Notes, and Practical Classroom Uses*. My work has always been deeply rooted in this idea—that you can use reading to teach writing. It's an idea whose time has come, as the exploding wealth of websites about mentor texts for teaching reading and writing clearly indicates.

Learning to use reading to teach writing means looking at readily available texts differently—like a writing thief. Most classrooms are equipped with libraries, so teachers have the resources right at their fingertips to consider texts as models of writing right along with what they contribute to reading. There's a wellspring of mentor texts right at their fingertips. But for those classrooms without libraries, the school and public library, the Internet, and the everyday texts in the world around us all work equally well. Finding resources is not the most challenging part of the process, but teasing out of these materials the specific skills to teach in writing can be more difficult and takes practice to master.

The process ultimately yields boundless results, however. A deep, thoughtful understanding of how text works creates an understanding of what good writers do and, in turn, provides options for them as they write. The beauty of teachers and students turning to texts in this manner is that the study is generative. That is, as a teacher, or in my role as a guest teacher these days, I might, for example, plan a series of lessons on Pam Muñoz Ryan's fiction chapter book *Becoming Naomi León* as a way of having my students discover that many of her paragraphs are short (typically two or three sentences each) because they contain dialogue, so a new paragraph is created each time there's a change of speaker. I might then use examples from the same text to teach students how to work with dialogue—in context and when it matters—and bring in excellent teaching about conventions as well.

But here's the cool thing: Just as I think I'm winding down with our look at conventions, my students, heads down like hounds on a trail as they read and read sections of the novel, often catch the scent of new hunts. "Why does she use Spanish and English words?" a student might ask, and off we go, using the same text to point out other passages with distinctive tones (voice), how the beginnings of chapters work to engage the reader (organization), and how smoothly the sentences read aloud (sentence fluency). And, of course, since Naomi creates a "splendid words" list in English and Spanish, there's a direct connection to word choice.

Students Develop Bigger Understandings From Authors, Not Assignments

A student who's taught how to think about how text is constructed by using mentor texts might notice, for example, that Pam Muñoz Ryan's nonfiction picture book *Hello Ocean* consists of 18 sentences that actually form one paragraph from beginning to end. This student might ask if it's OK to write a paragraph with 18 sentences. Instead of a yes or no answer or responding with a formula (e.g., a topic sentence plus three supporting details), a better solution is found in studying the writing and its context. Then, the student writer may determine that 18 sentences work because it's a picture book. Or, he or she might decide to consult additional nonfiction books before arriving at a conclusion about the length and structure of paragraphs. Regardless of his or her observation and conclusion, the student is thinking and engaging with text in a deep and thoughtful way, which is exactly the goal we have in mind.

Along the way, students discover, of course, that there's no correct formula for how long a paragraph should be or how many paragraphs should be written, period. Writers have to make those important decisions themselves based on what they're writing and how best to convey the idea. To tell students that a paper has five paragraphs before the idea is committed to paper is the exact opposite of what they need to know: that it varies. A student's paper just might have five paragraphs by the time it wraps up. Or it might not. It's hard to disagree with what a wise teacher once told me: "There's a big difference between a five-paragraph essay and an essay that has five paragraphs." For the sake of young writers everywhere, throw out the formulas and replace them with thinking activities that allow students to develop bigger understandings of how good writing works.

Do you have a classroom library? Do you have access to the public library and the Internet? Consider using those books and materials as mentor texts for teaching writing, right along with what they bring to reading instruction. They should become coteachers in your classroom and an infinite source of inspiration for lessons and activities that model the very best writing. Here's what I mean: Have you noticed that your students begin sentences the same way or with the same construction? Help them learn what sentence fluency is and how to use it more effectively in their own writing by turning to a paragraph or two out of a much admired text (fiction or nonfiction) and pointing out the varied sentence structures. Who's better to teach that lesson than Gary Paulsen in *Dogteam*, E.B. White in *Charlotte's Web*, Nicola Davies in *What's Eating You? Parasites—The Inside Story*, or J.K. Rowling in *Harry Potter and the Sorcerer's Stone*?

Here's another example: Are you concerned that your students' subject–verb agreement is erratic? Search several passages for examples of how this grammar construction is correctly handled in a text that students love, and point them out, discussing how the grammar principle works as you go. Then, invite students to find an example of this same

erb agreement issue in a piece of their own writing and note
's handled correctly. You already have these resources at your
Don't forget to draw from the world of writing around you
every day, too. Menus, brochures, signs, labels, advertisements, and so
forth make great mentor texts as well.

You won't find all the perfect models overnight, but honestly, the
books that teachers and students love have passages on every single page
that are worth studying for some quality of writing. Over time, your
resources for teaching writing will overflow just by noting how reading
serves to inspire writing. Students like this approach, and teachers do,
too. Why? Because print and nonprint are an infinite set of resources
that motivate and inspire. They are timely, topical, and a powerful way to
show students how writing works. And you don't need worksheets, lists
of words to memorize, and all the other dumb things we've inherited in
our teaching pedagogy over the years.

By using reading to teach writing, students who are unfamiliar with
English will benefit by becoming stronger readers and writers. They may
not know much about reading and writing when they begin, but if they're
seeing excellent examples of writing, reading them together, learning
how to talk about them, and applying this knowledge to their writing,
they'll be well on the way to English literacy. The aliterate students will
be motivated as well. How could they not want to read and write when
such wonderful models are filling up their literacy lives? Every student
in our nation's classrooms benefits from this approach to teaching and
learning.

Deep Reading: Linking Reading and Writing Processes

"Reading is like breathing in and writing is like breathing out," according
to Pam Allyn (2013, para. 5), a noted educational writer and researcher.
There's a symbiotic relationship between the two that benefits both.
When you write, you read back what you've said to see if the meaning
is clear, if it makes sense. You check off each of the traits in your
mind—ideas, organization, voice, word choice, sentence fluency, and
conventions—to make sure the text communicates your intent and is as
well crafted as possible. This is deep reading—close reading in its purest

form. It involves more than reading for general content; it means reading with the intent of discovering places that need further revision and editing so the final piece is crystal clear.

Deep reading also means slowing down to notice what the writer of a text that's not your own has done and why. This is when readers discover the techniques of the writer exhibited on the page. "Reading is a process of constructing meaning from the complex, naturally redundant network of syntactic, semantic, and graphophonic information that comprises written language," explains Bridges (2013, para. 7), a researcher and editor. Deep reading requires thinking about how the written language works.

Defined in *The Blackwell Encyclopedia of Writing Systems* (Coulmas, 1999), writing is the process of applying

> a set of visible or tactile signs used to represent units of language in a systematic way, with the purpose of recording messages which can be retrieved by everyone who knows the language in question and the rules by virtue of which its units are encoded in the writing system. (p. 560)

The retrieval, of course, is reading. In this respect, reading and writing are a one-two punch. When we work on the skills related to one, we quite naturally work on the other. I believe that one of our foremost tasks as writing teachers is to make the relationship transparent for students so they can see the influence that reading has on their writing and not leave it up to chance or a happy accident that a technique or idea from writing might show up in their own work.

Deep reading as a writer is something that students need help to understand. When I interviewed fourth-grade students in Blue Springs, Missouri, on this topic, one student came to understand a different way of looking at reading by zeroing in on one of the traits, organization:

Me: Devon, would you talk about how you learn about writing by what you are reading?

Devon: I don't know what you mean.

Me: Do you ever read something that you really like and wind up trying to do something like it in your writing?

Devon: Oh. So, like when Mrs. Gaines just read *The One and Only Ivan* (I really liked that book), I could write a story about a gorilla or a zoo or something?

Me:	Sorta. I was thinking more about how the book was written, not just what it was about. Did Katherine Applegate do anything interesting in her writing that helped you relate to the idea?
Devon:	[pause] Hmm…I don't know.
Me:	Let's get a copy of the book and see if you can find something in it that really worked for you as a reader. Then, let's look at it like writers and see what she did to make you feel that way.
Devon:	OK.

Devon and I thumbed through the book together. He pointed out how the text was spaced generously on the page (presentation), making it easy to read. He noted that the chapter titles weren't capitalized (conventions), and we talked about the effect of that editing decision on the reader. Less than three minutes into discussing the book and paging through it, he pointed to a line on page 160 and read aloud, "This handprint can't be so easily wiped away."

Devon:	This line is good. I think it's important.
Me:	How so?
Devon:	It's kinda saying that Ivan doesn't feel important, but a handprint makes him feel like one of a kind, like the title says.
Me:	An interesting connection, Devon. I wonder if other chapters are organized to end on notes like this, helping the reader think deeply about what happened and what it means.
Devon:	[after looking for less than a minute] Here's another one, page 120: "When I gaze at the food-court skylight, the moon Stella loved is shrouded in clouds." That's really sad. That happens after Stella dies. I was really mad at Mack in that part.
Me:	So, when Stella dies, Applegate could have written, "It was really sad, and I felt terrible," as a chapter ending, but she wrote the one you like instead. What's the difference?
Devon:	Well, um…the way the real author does it makes me feel terrible for Ivan, and I felt terrible, too. Your ending would be kinda boring, no offense.

Me: [laughing] None taken. But how great is this? Just think about what you noticed: One way of writing the chapter ending is more interesting and makes a connection to you as a reader. Let's look through your writing from Mrs. Gaines's class and see if there is a place in one where you can do what Applegate does: make a connection to the reader by writing something more thoughtful and important than just a boring ending. That's putting the organization trait to work for you. It will improve the voice in your writing, too, just like it did in *The One and Only Ivan*.

We spent the next several minutes looking at endings to Devon's pieces. He chose a short journal entry that ended, "And finally we did magnets in science class today," to revise. I noticed that as he considered what to write, he went back to Applegate's text and looked at different chapter endings for inspiration. That's the organization trait. Devon wasn't writing about the same topic of the book, of course, but he came to understand that the moves Applegate makes at the end of her chapters could inspire his own endings. His final choice was, "Science is not usually the best time of the day, but today working with magnets was the polar opposite." How clever and a real improvement in voice! In a short, focused conference, Devon came to realize that reading could help him improve his writing in ways he'd never considered before. And now he's off and running with his newly learned strategy.

My Summer Ritual

I think all writers are affected by their reading. I have a summer ritual of reading *To Kill a Mockingbird* by Harper Lee; I've done this for more than 15 years. I'm not sure how it started, but when August rolls around, I hunt for a new copy of the book at my local bookstore—a different edition than I already own in hardcover or paperback because I'm a collector, too— and I read. When I tell students about my August reading habit, they always ask, "Why?" They wonder why anyone would read a book, a hard, old book, that many times. The answer is easy: It hasn't finished teaching me yet—neither the message nor Lee's magnificent writing. Moreover, although I find the book to be warm and funny, it's also powerful and horrifying, a combination that I find compelling as a reader.

About the third or fourth reading, I started noticing things about the writing style. I saw how the book was really a series of vignettes of life in imaginary Macomb, Alabama, during the Great Depression of the late 1930s to the mid-1940s; the individual stories were artfully seamed together to create the novel.

Each reading, I study the passages that have a specific tone and how they combine to create the overall voice of the piece. I see how Lee reveals information deliberately, using carefully placed details to maximize their impact. I notice how one chapter is paced slowly to help me understand the intent of the passage: the part where the ladies of Macomb society have tea, and Scout, the motherless, free-spirited youngster, is initiated into the women's world. Those pages remind me of Jane Austen and how she writes about the subtleties of society, which led me one year to an Austen reading spree and falling for Mr. Darcy all over again. In Lee's text, I notice, too, how the pace of the writing picks up in other scenes, especially those in which Tom Robinson is the focus. I'm mesmerized by the complexity of Lee's sentences and how she constructs them, as I realize that each one was the result of a conscious effort to revise until it sounded just right. I'm convinced that there's not a line in her book that's the same as in the first draft.

Great writing happens in books such as *To Kill a Mockingbird*, when the writer relates real information about what he or she knows and what he or she understands to be true with stunning authority and authenticity. In Lee's case, it's growing up in the South, the Great Depression, the society of women, racial inequality and cruelties, class structure, mental health, and the journey toward integrity and honesty. Although I didn't grow up in Macomb in the late 1930s, I relate to the issues in the book and add Lee's perspective about them to my own worldview.

> 66 Well-written nonfiction is literature and can have the same profound effect on readers as fiction. 99

This is just as true in nonfiction writing. Well-written nonfiction is literature and can have the same profound effect on readers as fiction. Information goes through the writer's sieve and is made accessible for the reader through the compelling voice of the author—whether in story or information or both—and becomes a part of you, the reader. Through his or her ideas and voice, the author teaches you how to process the world and make sense of it. This is the power of reading. It changes you. You're a different person when you close the book (or turn off your tablet) than when you started it. And you're a better reader and writer. What's interesting to note if you're a writing teacher is *how* the author managed to get into your head and heart and which ideas and techniques are worth stealing from him or her to show student writers. This practice of examining mentor texts can become one of the pleasures of our job: carefully scrutinizing the writing to understand how writers make their moves and stealing their best techniques to try on our own.

Traits: The Language of Writers

To help students dig into text and move past "I really liked it" or "I didn't like it at all," we need a language to describe what's going on in the writing that all stakeholders know and understand. We need to be on the same page when we talk about reading so we can get past the surface and discuss the writing and how it works in detail. I suggest using the traits. They're simple and straightforward, and in their 25+ years of being out in the world, helping writing teachers teach, they're surprisingly uncontroversial.

Having common terminology for talking about and working with writing doesn't seem like a revolutionary idea, but I'm always surprised that many schools and classroom teachers don't take advantage of what using the same language brings to teaching and learning in writing. In fact, every other discipline has this: math, science, reading, and all others. Each content area has commonly used and understood terminology that cuts across the school years. Math has vocabulary such as *addition, subtraction, multiplication,* and *division*. Science uses process terms such as *variable, hypothesize, data, predict, classify,* and *investigation*. In reading, we use terms such as *context, details, inference, text complexity,* and *summary*. Writing has the traits: ideas, organization, voice, word choice, sentence fluency, conventions, and presentation. The consistency of language among and between grades provides the ability to map the writing curriculum so it deepens from year to year. From random scribbling on the page to artfully crafted essays, stories, and writing in every possible format, the traits are the common denominator to ensure continuity for writers of all ages.

have been in the writing teacher's assessment and
ol kit for more than 25 years. Indeed, I've spent a good
reer developing books and materials to use the traits for
nd instruction. Recently, I added key qualities to each trait so
systematically break down the specific skills that students
n in order to write a solid piece, regardless of the purpose.
These key qualities are what we look for as we assess writing, trait by
trait, and based on what we find, the key qualities become the targets of
further instruction. In this way, assessment and instruction become two
sides of the same coin.

Do
we
use?

The Key Qualities for Each Writing Trait

Ideas: The piece's content

- *Finding a topic:* The piece has a clear, central theme or a simple, original story line that is memorable. If the piece has a title, that title captures that theme or story line in an enticing way.

- *Focusing the topic:* The writer has narrowed a big issue or thesis to a reasonable, manageable topic or distilled the story to a clear, tight narrative.

- *Developing the topic:* The writer provides enough critical evidence to support the issue or thesis and shows insight on the topic, or tells the story in a fresh way. The ideas transcend the obvious and predictable.

- *Using details:* The details create pictures in the reader's mind and are plentiful from beginning to end. The writer's knowledge about and/or experience with the topic is evident through the use of accurate details, credible information, and believable anecdotes.

Organization: The internal structure of the piece

- *Creating the lead:* The beginning grabs the reader's attention and leads him or her into the piece naturally. The beginning entices the reader to keep reading, providing a tantalizing glimpse of what is to come.

- *Using sequence and transition words:* The piece contains a variety of carefully selected sequence and transition words, which are placed wisely to guide the reader through the text by showing how ideas progress, relate, and/or diverge.

- *Developing the body:* The piece is easy to follow because the details fit together logically. The writer slows down to spotlight important points or events and speeds up when he or she needs to keep the reader moving along.
- *Ending with a sense of resolution:* The writer sums up his or her thinking in a natural, thoughtful, and convincing way and has anticipated and answered any lingering questions, giving the reader a strong sense of closure.

Voice: The tone and tenor of the piece

- *Establishing a tone:* The piece shows how much the writer cares about the topic. The piece is expressive and compelling, whereby the reader feels the writer's conviction, authority, and integrity.
- *Conveying the purpose:* The reason for writing is clear. The writer expresses his or her point of view appropriately for the form (narrative, expository, persuasive, or other), which adds interest to the overall message.
- *Creating a connection to the audience:* There is a strong interaction between the reader and the writer. The writer has considered what the reader needs to know and the best way to convey it by sharing his or her feelings and opinions about the topic.
- *Taking risks to create voice:* The writer expresses ideas in new ways, which makes the piece interesting, original, and fresh. The writing sounds like the writer because of the particular use of words and phrases that have a "just right" effect.

Word choice: The vocabulary the writer uses to convey meaning and enlighten the reader

- *Using strong verbs:* The piece contains many action words, giving it punch and pizzazz. The writer has stretched to find lively verbs that add energy to the piece.
- *Using striking words and phrases:* The piece contains many finely honed words and phrases that make it stand out. The writer employs creative and effective use of alliteration, similes, metaphors, and/or other literary techniques.
- *Using words that are specific and accurate:* The words are precise, often reflecting content- or information-based vocabulary that the reader needs to understand the message fully. The writer has chosen nouns,

adjectives, adverbs, and so forth that create clarity and bring the topic to life.

- *Using language effectively:* The words have been selected to capture the reader's imagination and enhance the piece's meaning. A deliberate attempt to choose the best word over the first word that comes to mind is evident.

Sentence fluency: The way words and phrases flow through the piece

- *Capturing smooth and rhythmic flow:* The writer has thought about how the sentences sound. If the piece were to be shared aloud, it would be easy on the ear. The writer uses phrasing that sounds almost musical and is therefore a joy to read.

- *Crafting well-built sentences:* The sentences are carefully and creatively constructed for maximum impact. Transition words such as *but*, *and*, and *so* are used successfully to join sentences and sentence parts.

- *Varying sentence patterns:* A variety of sentence types (simple, compound, and/or complex) enhances the central theme or story line. The piece is made up of an effective mix of long, complex sentences and short, simple ones.

- *Breaking the "rules" to create fluency:* If the piece contains fragments, they add style. The writer may use one word to accent a particular moment, such as, "Bam!" If the writer uses a conversational tone, the sentences might begin with informal words such as *well*, *and*, or *but*. The writer breaks rules intentionally to make that dialogue sound authentic.

Conventions: The mechanical correctness of the piece

- *Checking spelling:* Sight words, high-frequency words, and even less familiar words are usually spelled correctly. When less familiar words are spelled incorrectly, they are phonetically correct. Overall, the piece shows control in spelling.

- *Using punctuation and indenting paragraphs:* The writer handles basic punctuation skillfully. He or she understands how to use punctuation to add clarity and style. Paragraphs are indented in the right places. The piece is ready for a general audience.

- *Inserting capitalization:* The use of capital letters is consistent and accurate. An in-depth understanding of how to capitalize dialogue, abbreviations, proper names, and titles is evident.

- *Applying grammar and usage:* Words and their prefixes and suffixes have been combined to form grammatically correct phrases and sentences. The writer shows care in using the correct grammar and usage. The writer may break rules of Standard English for stylistic reasons but otherwise shows consistency and control.

Presentation: The physical appearance of the piece

- *Applying handwriting skills:* The handwriting, whether printed or cursive, is clear and legible. Letters are uniform and slant evenly throughout. The spacing between words is consistent.

- *Using word processing:* The font style and size are easy to read and a good match for the piece's purpose. If color is used, it enhances the piece's readability.

- *Using white space:* Appropriately sized margins frame the text. There are no cross-outs, smudges, or tears in the paper.

- *Incorporating text features:* Text features are effectively placed on the page and clearly align with the text that they support.

How Getting Granular Yields Better Mentor Text Mining—and More Focused Teaching

It's necessary to break the trait domains down into smaller, understandable, and teachable key qualities to provide the consistency and continuity for teaching that's critical to scaling up over the years. Instead of saying, "I'm teaching the ideas trait," try this instead: "I'm teaching students how to focus and narrow their topics within the ideas trait." It's more specific, it's concrete, and we can develop lessons and activities that support student learning and make a noticeable difference in their writing.

Of course, we'll also find it easier to locate mentor texts if we know exactly what issue we're looking to nail down. The search is on for mentor texts that show each of the key qualities, trait by trait, in exemplar pieces of writing. I've provided a whole wealth of possibilities for you in the chapters that follow.

As discussed here and in Chapter 1, shared vocabulary is important. The traits provide the language we use in the writing classroom to systematically teach the craft. The key qualities make it just that much easier to zero in on what to teach within each trait. "To name it is to tame it," as epistemologist Jeremy Sherman (2010, para. 12) says. If we can name what isn't working in writing, we can tame that same quality in our work with students. Conversely, if we can name what makes the work strong, we can encourage students to continue doing it. We learn by repetition, after all, so learning to write well means doing some things well over and over to build toward success at deeper and more complex levels.

Having a language that all writers share is key to this process. The key qualities of the traits provide much needed help in this effort, along with models or mentor texts. We look to them for examples of successful practices, name them, and then try them out as they help guide our thinking toward complex, clear, coherent text.

How Do You Spot a Mentor Text?

I used to focus on collecting picture books as mentor texts and sought ways to align the texts to one or more of the traits. It was an excellent excuse to expand my personal library of picture books, something I really enjoy not only as a writer but as a children's book aficionado as well. In the past few years, however, I've thrown open the mentor text doors and invited in short passages from longer texts and everyday texts that are equally useful for teaching. Mentor texts can be materials that the student writer discovers on his or her own, such as how chapter endings are written in *The One and Only Ivan*, or something the teacher shares with students to showcase a particular skill in context, such as how a restaurant menu description for a hamburger sounds mouthwateringly tasty by using striking words and phrases.

The reason these resources are mentor texts is that we learn something about writing from them, not just what an amazing story *The One and Only Ivan* is or how much we want to bite into that hamburger at the local restaurant. For these two widely divergent texts to become true mentor texts, they must spark our writer's curiosity and be studied for their techniques so we figure out how they can be applied to our own work to make it just as memorable. It's a different way to think about reading and writing.

Using mentor texts in the classroom just makes sense. But there's a catch. To find the right ones, you have to have resources from which to select. In other words, to be a writing thief, you'll have to case the joint to figure out what to pilfer. Think about the resources that are readily available in your classroom, in the library, in print and nonprint resources right at your fingertips every day. Don't make this hard. Good writing is everywhere; you just need to see reading through the eyes of the writer.

You also have to love the selections you choose—love them enough that you can return to them over and over again, each time finding something new about the writing to talk about and try. That's a pretty tall order. It won't work for you to try to sell your students on a list of books and materials that I love. It's absolutely critical that you find and fall in love with them together. They have to speak to all of you as readers and writers. You can, however, steal my list and ideas from this book and other trait-based resources and use them as a launching pad of what to look for and what to try. But to become a true writing thief, you'll need to make finding your own mentor texts a new priority in your everyday teaching practice.

I'm pretty sure that many readers aren't as inspired by *To Kill a Mockingbird* as I am; I believe I could teach a whole year of writing from that book, even to elementary-age students. I believe it, so I could do it. I'd draw on the social studies curriculum, and we'd understand more about that time and place in U.S. history as well as how writers create Pulitzer Prize–winning novels. But I could do the same thing with any text that's written well enough, and so can you. You just have to see the possibilities.

There's an art and an intuition to finding the right texts. Author and researcher Ray (1999) says,

> The bottom line for why I select a text is that I see something in how that text is written which would be useful for my students to also see. I see something about the text that holds potential for my students' learning. I am looking for texts that have something in them or about them that can add to my students' knowledge base of how to write well. (p. 188)

Here's my challenge to you: What have you read lately that you loved? Was it Nicola Davies's brilliant nonfiction book *Deadly! The Truth About the Most Dangerous Creatures on Earth* or perhaps the book that

Figure 3. Pizzacato Loves Its Pizza

i heart pizza

the driver of this car ADORES PIZZA. IN FACT, EVERYONE WHO WORKS AT PIZZICATO LIVES, BREATHES AND DREAMS ABOUT PIZZA. WE'RE A QUIRKY BUNCH... BUT WE EAT WELL.

Note. Photo courtesy of Tracy Frankel, founder and president of Pizzacato Pizza.

I haven't stopped thinking about since I read it recently, *Wonder* by R.J. Palacio? Maybe you were behind a pizza delivery car in Portland, Oregon, and read the text shown in Figure 3. How can you not want to drop everything and go to Pizzacato Pizza for a little lunch? The genuine love that these folks have for their pizza comes through in the voice of their brilliant marketing.

When I find something like this, I feel a rush of energy, a thrill of excitement—a frisson. A discovery like this is gold. I can use it in teaching to show why writing shouldn't be dull or boring. According to Murray (1997), voice "may be the most important element in writing. It supports and extends what the writer says" (p. 10). I couldn't agree more. There's a reason the top-level exemplars posted from state and national assessments score high in voice. This trait of writing, a primary trait, is often what separates great writing from proficient pieces. And although proficiency may be a goal for test taking, we should have a higher goal for student writers: excellence.

Seek the frisson. When you discover a mentor text, you should feel excitement and energy, a thrill or rush from the words and the way the author conveys the ideas. That's a frisson—that tingly sensation you feel when something is just right. When you and your students find a passage in a picture book, brochure, sign, blog, website, e-mail, advertisement, television show, movie, play, or song lyric, you'll feel the frisson: Voila! You've found a great mentor text! Beg, borrow, or steal it to help students learn about writing and how important it is that their work stands out in a similar way. Help them find their writing voices and develop their craft with mentor texts.

AUTHOR INSIGHTS: *Nicola Davies*

 It wasn't until I began to teach writing (I was a lecturer in creative writing at Bath Spa University for six years) that I realized that I knew how to write in the way that a potter knows how to shape a bowl or a carpenter knows how to make dovetail joints. Looking at other people's writing, and knowing what they had to do to fix it, made me see that I actually had skills.

I know that seems silly, because I'd already written a number of books for children and adults by then, but having to analyze students' work made me think about and articulate my own practice to myself. It made me see that all the reading I had done in my life—much of it at the formative stages of adolescence and early adulthood—had taught me my craft. I knew what good writing was and what my taste in words was because I had read good stuff. My family was not wealthy or upper class: My father was the first person in his family to go to university, and my grandfathers' families were miners, steelworkers, and small holders, but they were Welsh, and in Welsh culture, there is a huge store set by literature. So, my father recited Keats to me—I can see him now shaving and saying, "Season on mists and mellow fruitfulness..."—and my mother bought me books, such as Hardy's complete works for my 16th birthday. I don't think I read any contemporary fiction before I was 25. I was a hugely snobby reader of just "great works" by Hardy, Eliot, André Gide, Albert Camus, Tolstoy, etc., etc. (although weirdly not Dickens, whom I've come to in later life) and lots of 19th-century romantic and First World War poetry, which I loved and still love. That was the reading that shaped my writing; that's what made words matter to me so much, so that now I test everything I write by reading it aloud, and I want it to sound good, to feel good in the mouth as it's spoken, as well as to convey my chosen messages.

Specifically, as a nonfiction author, it's poetry that was my biggest influence—the animal poems of D.H. Lawrence (I hate his fiction with a passion, but his writing about animals is clear and true and honest), Ted Hughes, Wordsworth, Keats, Les Murray, Kathleen Jamie...I could go on and on. Most people don't realize that most poetry is observational nonfiction (Wordsworth's description of a skylark is perfectly accurate as well as being an emotional silver bullet), that it delivers sensory and emotional experience about the world in an easy-to-carry narrative package. I say *narrative* because I see narrative not as "story" as it's often represented but as a piece of writing that has a memorable shape and feel, a kind of manageable carrier for the information it contains.

As for what I read when I'm getting ready to write—well, nothing that has much to do with the writing itself. That kind of reading is something that's been going on all my life. So, my reading for a nonfiction book is all about the information: scientific papers, textbooks—also increasingly anthropological and cultural information as I'm more and more interested in writing things that more obviously address the relationship of humans and the natural world, and the meanings that our contact with nature has for us. At the level of book-specific influences, visual art is probably my greatest source of inspiration—my way of finding the narrative thread.

Notes From Ruth

I'm spellbound by Davies's writing. The notion that poetry is "observational nonfiction" has haunted me since the first time I read her words. It's no wonder that I have the same reaction every time I read a book by this author: Each is lyrical, musical, elegant. The line between informational and narrative writing is certainly blurred by her, which is why her work is so extraordinary to use as mentor texts. You can write factually but beautifully. Students need to know that.

In Chapter 3, we'll explore informational texts and how to use them to help students develop skills in each of the traits. By sharing examples of mentor texts in a specific mode, you'll see how the traits and modes work together: the how (traits) and the what (modes/purposes) of writing. You'll hear more from published authors of children's books about how reading affects their writing. Best of all, I'll help you steal lots of flat-out awesome mentor texts to inspire students to write informational texts, and I include ideas for how to use them with student writers.

CHAPTER 3

Informational Writing

*a*s I'm gathering (and sometimes pilfering) books and materials as exemplars to recommend as mentor texts, it's clear that the purpose for writing (the mode) influences how each of the traits operates within those texts. To maximize what mentor texts can bring to teaching and learning, we need to focus on the modes of writing right along with the traits. Simply put, the traits are *how* to write (ideas, organization, voice, word choice, sentence fluency, conventions, and presentation), and the modes are *what* we write (informational, narrative, or argument [opinion]). In this chapter, we'll explore the informational mode through the lens of each trait, and then in subsequent chapters, we'll focus on narrative and opinion writing, respectively.

In this Common Core State Standards era, the purposes for writing have taken center stage. As you recall, the first group of Writing Anchor Standards in the Common Core relates to text types and purposes (narrative, informational/explanatory, and argument in diverse print and electronic formats). Writing should always be purpose driven and well crafted. The traits and the modes work hand in hand. With that in mind, we must apply an additional filter in our search for mentor texts: purpose/ modes. It's not enough to seek mentor texts that show strength in each of the traits, as they must be exemplars of the mode as well. The following are simple definitions of the modes or purposes for writing:

- *Narrative:* To tell a story

- *Informational:* To explain, describe, or inform

- *Argument (opinion):* To convince using logic and reason

But there's more to the purpose for writing than these core definitions reveal. Don't we also write to entertain and dazzle? To connect or reconnect? To figure something out and learn? To challenge and call to action? To feel, laugh out loud, and cry? And much more? These are also purposes that we have in mind when we write to tell a story, inform, or construct an argument, so although there may be three main purposes for writing, within the text of each lies the potential to reach the reader through a secondary set of purposes, too. It's for these additional reasons that writers write and readers read.

In this chapter, I focus on informational mentor texts that inform, explain, describe, or define the subject for the reader in such a way that is credible, clear, and captivating. I included the last three descriptors to make sure an informational mentor text stands the test of literature—that as a piece of writing, it is solid because of artistic merit. Informational writing is literature when it's well written, just as its narrative counterpart strives to be.

Writing to inform and explain has traditionally been labeled "expository," but the Common Core uses the terms *informational/explanatory*. It could be confusing to use all three terms in this chapter, so I settled on *informational*. Common language is a foundational principal for my work with the traits all these years, so now that the purposes are a big part of the professional dialogue, too, it seems logical to find that same thread to pull through this work as well.

What Makes Informational Writing Tick?

Informational writing can be brilliantly written right along with providing solid, credible information. Here's a piece to prove the point from *At Large and at Small: Familiar Essays* by Anne Fadiman (2007), writer and observer of the scientific world. In this example from her essay, "Ice Cream," she explores the different ways of making ice cream:

> In the brave new world of nitro, no ice cream maker, either hand-crank or electric, is necessary. If the mix has been pre-chilled in a kitchen freezer, liquid nitrogen freezes it so fast that one needs only a metal pot and a metal stirring spoon (glass or plastic would shatter). I have frequently witnessed the process, which can justly be described as Macbethian. Because liquid nitrogen boils at 320 degrees below zero, when it comes into contact with warm air and is forced to change from a liquid to a gas, it seethes and steams like water in a spaghetti pot. (p. 57)

Anne Fadiman's (2007) informational writing is far more than a recitation of facts and information told in an impersonal voice. Instead, she uses her curiosity about ice cream—its history and mouthwatering allure—to pique our interest. She makes the topic interesting by using facts written with precision and poetry that keep us reading, marveling at each new revelation, while we savor the lyrical way the text is written.

Here's my point: Informational writing has gotten a bad rap. It should be a thrilling joy ride to explore new ideas through facts and details. Good informational writing should not read like a textbook or an encyclopedia entry; it should read like literature. It should *be* literature. As teachers, we ought to be dancing in the streets that there are now so many stellar informational texts to share with our student writers. These are the texts that belong in the classroom and in our lesson plans for writing, reading, and content area learning. And any text that we ourselves thinks is old school, deadly dull, should be run out of town in the next faculty meeting. When I visit schools all around the country, I'm a rabble rouser, telling teachers that they need to have a collective voice and prove the difference between teaching with engaging texts and disengaging ones.

> 66 Good informational writing should not read like a textbook or an encyclopedia entry; it should read like literature. It should *be* literature. 99

Let it be known to our students, too, that authors of effective informational writing don't just present facts. There's no quicker way to turn off readers than by boring them to death or trying to impress them with how much you know. If you really know a lot about something, chances are that it started out as a simple interest that grew over time and circumstance to a full-fledged fascination. The energy behind that process of discovery should fill every page. Without it, the writing will be lackluster and forgettable.

I'm reminded of my friend Bridey's youngest son, Dominic. From the time he was old enough to write and draw, he wrote about the airlines: stories, information sheets, and opinion pieces about which airline was best. He read everything he could find about the airlines, reading far above his prescribed Lexile level. He talked nonstop about the airlines, often explaining to me which plane I'd likely be on for my next trip, how many seats it had, and which were best located for comfort. He knew which concourses at our local airport were equipped for the biggest planes and which could only handle the smaller ones. If you needed an expert on the airlines, Dominic was your man. Once, he did a video commercial for one of the airlines and sent it in to them, hoping it would air on television. I'm sure it's still out there on YouTube somewhere.

Dominic was obsessed by the airlines. His teachers commented that his passion for his topic made his writing stand out in his class and across the school. And it did. There was no doubt that Dominic's writing was coming along faster than many of his peers' until fourth grade, when the teacher insisted he write about her topics and forbid him from writing about the airlines the rest of the year. So, he just stopped writing. What was a strength and source of joy for him at school turned into worksheets and predictable topics, which stunted his writing growth. Dominic is just beginning college now, but that joy of writing (and reading) never returned. He still loves airlines, though, and one day his career will be in that industry because that is where his passion lies.

This is what I've learned: When we write about things that matter to us, it provides us with the courage and momentum to keep going. Think about how hard it is to write well. There are no shortcuts, no way to tiptoe through the revision process. It must be a full-on romp. Writing includes many failures and, if we really work at it, some extraordinary successes. If we want students to understand this and embrace it, we have to let them choose what they write and help them find the frissons that will carry them through the hard parts. In other words, they have to want to write before they can write well—fiction or nonfiction.

> Motivation is at the heart of writing. If nonfiction is where you do your best writing, or your best teaching of writing, don't be buffaloed into the idea that it's an inferior species. The only important distinction is between good writing and bad writing. Good writing is good writing, whatever form it takes and whatever we call it. (Zinsser, 2006, p. 99)

In the last decade, nonfiction reading and writing has been a huge focus for educators at every level. Understanding that much of what is read and written as adults is nonfiction, the push is on to develop strategies for teaching and using nonfiction in classrooms as we prepare students for college and the workplace. I applaud this effort, although I think we should include preparation for life as a goal, too. As an adult, I read mostly fiction. Fiction keeps me up late at night, reading into the early morning hours, prowling a bookstore for another book by the same author, or wishing the plane wouldn't land so I can finish one more chapter. Fiction has power over me. I'm drawn to it. Ironically, I write nonfiction, so being a writing thief, I've stolen a lot of writing techniques from fiction authors that show up in my work. Ultimately, I agree with William Zinsser that good writing is good writing; we can learn from every well-written book, magazine article, brochure, sign, or any one of hundreds of other informational text types.

Informational Writing Reveals Big Thinking

Informational writing is primarily nonfiction. Its main purpose is to relay facts and information in a cohesive and thoughtful way by using formats such as essays, books, journals, blogs, brochures, how-to manuals, signs, and lists. If you think of informational writing as the Common Core (NGA Center & CCSSO, 2010a) defines it—"to examine and convey complex ideas and information clearly and accurately through the effective selection, organization, and analysis of content" (p. 18)—then you'll recognize that there's a never-ending source of possible formats to organize a never-ending list of "big thinking" informational topics.

Nonfiction is a genre (category) of prose that includes but is not exclusive to informational writing. You'll also find nonfiction in the narrative world as memoirs, journals, diaries, biographies, and so forth—stories that the author relays factually but uses a narrative structure to do so. I'll address narrative writing structure in Chapter 4.

I really like this definition of what makes informational writing strong:

> Exposition is a type of oral or written discourse that is used to explain, describe, give information or inform. The creator of an expository text can not assume that the reader or listener has prior knowledge or prior understanding of the topic that is being discussed. One important point to keep in mind for the author is to try to use words that clearly show what they are talking about rather then [sic] blatantly telling the reader what is being discussed. Since clarity requires strong organization, one of the most important mechanisms that can be used to improve our skills in exposition is to provide directions to improve the organization of the text. (Expository Writing Program, n.d., para. 1)

Notice how the author of this definition addresses key issues embedded in informational text while weaving in several traits: ideas, organization, and word choice. I'm certain that if this definition were expanded, it would include the other traits as well because, in the simplest of terms, the mode (purpose) is *what* we write, and the traits are *how* the writing is crafted. They work together hand in hand.

Here's part of a newspaper article that I stole from the pocket of an airplane seat, left by a previous passenger last summer while traveling. It's an informational piece, no question. But notice how the author focuses on one of the traits (organization) and the key quality of creating the lead to entice the reader.

> Most interesting man in the world, meet your match.
>
> This week Twitter user Matthew Barrett created something of a sensation by linking to the obscure Wikipedia biography of the British army officer Sir Adrian Carton de Wiart. His tweet—"This guy surely has the best opening paragraph of any Wikipedia biography ever"—has been retweeted more than 3,200 times during the past several days.
>
> So just how mind-blowing is the introduction on Carton de Wiart's page? Judge for yourself:
>
> *Lieutenant-General Sir Adrian Paul Ghislain Carton de Wiart VC, KBE, CB, CMG, DSO (5 May 1880 - 5 June 1963), was a British Army officer of Belgian and Irish descent. He fought in the Boer War, World War I, and World War II, was shot in the face, head, stomach, ankle, leg, hip and ear, survived a plane crash, tunneled out of a POW camp, and bit off his own fingers when a doctor wouldn't amputate them. He later said "frankly I had enjoyed the war."* (Groll, 2013, paras. 1–4)

So, it's true. Informational writing does not need to be dull, boring, and merely a recitation of facts. It should reveal the big thinking behind the idea by intriguing the reader with facts and information that show how much the writer really knows and has thought about the idea. Informational text's primary purpose is to use information to enlighten readers, which, when done well, has the effect of spellbinding the reader every bit as much as a great narrative. In trait terms, we'd call that voice. Writers need to do more than replicate sources in this mode; they should strive to transform facts and information so the text fulfills the purpose for writing, so it becomes something new that reveals the idea with a fresh and original perspective. To move student writers to this deeper and more complex thinking about informational writing, we must find the right examples to show them how magnificent informational writing can and should be so they can steal the writer's moves to try in their own writing.

Perhaps it is because I am a librarian by trade—although I've been writing full time now for nearly a decade—but I simply can't sit down to write without reading and researching first. One might not anticipate this revelation from a picture book author, but it is truer than you could possibly guess. Please join me in looking at some current projects, and you'll understand how and why reading influences me as a writer.

Most recently, I have written and published a series of books about baby animals and their families with Hyperion: *Stay Close to Mama* (2012), *Just Like My Papa* (2013), and *My Bibi Always Remembers* (2014). Illustrator Mike Wohnoutka brilliantly captures in paint what I try to evoke in words—the wide East African savannah and the animals that call it home. But how to adequately achieve that miracle of words that will transport you there? How do I capture the endless, grassy plains; the deep, muddy waterholes; the vast, starlit skies? Can I depend only on my memories of travel there? Hardly so!

No, instead I ferry home huge armloads of books from the public library—books about giraffes, about lions, about elephants. I read and read, sinking into the silence of my writing cottage and making my way across time zones and continents until the words in those volumes bring to life the graceful, loping, six-foot baby giraffe; the deep-throated rumble of the lion's roar in the darkest night; the nearly silent swish of an elephant family through the swaying grass. I read and read, gulping down the words that will paint the memories, grant me the understanding, supply me the power to form my own perfect words. I cannot write without reading, nor would I want to. Reading and writing are two sides of a fountain that feeds my soul, the waters comingled from moment to moment and inseparable.

Notes From Ruth

Toni Buzzeo is one of my favorite picture book authors. She won me over years ago with the extensive research that she undertakes before writing. I think this is an area that students don't fully understand about writing. They look at a beautifully written and illustrated picture book, such as *My Bibi Always Remembers,* and think the author sat down on a Sunday afternoon and just merrily jotted it down, in finished form. That's not how it works, of course, as Toni clearly points out. I really appreciate the emphasis that she makes on research and how reading and writing are two sides of the same coin. Her works show the care she takes to get the information right.

The Traits and Informational Writing

What follows are definitions of the traits and how each works within the mode of informational writing. The traits are present in every form of writing, every time you write, but they take on a particular spin based on the purpose for the writing. In this case, we're looking at mentor texts that are in the informational mode as I defined earlier: their purpose is to inform, explain, describe, or define the subject for the reader in such a way that is credible, clear, and captivating. The more we understand about what we're writing (the purpose/mode), the easier it is to jump in and sort out how the piece will be written (the traits).

The Ideas Trait and Informational Writing

Ideas: The piece's content—its central message and details that support that message

A powerful idea in informational writing delves into what really matters about the topic. It tells the story of that idea, even without a narrative structure. It weaves facts into the running account, staying on point. It offers an insider's perspective that shows the writer's commitment and fascination with the topic. This is why it's necessary for writers to have ownership of their topics; it's hard to write with conviction using someone else's idea.

Informational writing conveys information accurately and reliably and increases the reader's understanding of a topic. It explains what the reader needs to know for the topic to make sense. It's clear and focused and provides more than superficial details; it includes unexpected or surprising details using facts and referring to primary and secondary sources as needed.

One of the keys to success in informational writing is that it anticipates and answers the reader's questions. That means the writer considers the audience and includes information in "just right" doses so the topic will fascinate and intrigue the reader as well.

Getting Started With Mentor Texts

I recommend the following mentor texts to help students understand how informational writing appears when you zero in on each of the traits and its four key qualities. Consider this a starter list that will likely make you realize, Oh, I have a book just like this in my classroom library, or, The next time I go to my favorite restaurant, I'll nab a copy of their menu because it's so cleverly written. The secret to being a world-class writing thief is knowing what you're looking for and realizing that resources for teaching are everywhere. You don't have to have every one of these specific books or materials to embrace this way of thinking, by the way. But that being said, the ones listed here are pretty great!

Getting Into the Informational State of Mind

Written Anything Good Lately?
written by Susan Allen and Jane Lindaman,
illustrated by Vicky Enright
Millbrook, 2006

This simple alphabet book is ideal for helping students understand the variety of text types to choose from when they're writing in the informational mode. The ideas for writing are arranged in alphabetical order from A to Z and include short writing pieces, such as kudos to a classmate, and longer pieces, such as a report on the rain forests.

The pictures that accompany the simple list of ideas are delightful and expressive, making the reader feel that any of these writing options will be enjoyable along with informational. You can read this book together and brainstorm more text types for informational writing. Post the ideas or put them on cards in an easy-to-use system, such as on a ring or in an index card box, and encourage students to consider the options in prewriting when they pick text types and formats for their writing. Leave this book out. It will find the right readers and writers at the right time.

Mentor Texts and the Ideas Trait

Key Quality: *Finding a Topic.* The writer offers a clear, central theme or a simple, original story line that is memorable.

Manfish: A Story of Jacques Cousteau
written by Jennifer Berne, illustrated by Éric Puybaret
Chronicle, 2008

What could be a better model than this text for finding a topic? Not only does this picture book provide a good biography of Cousteau's life as a world-class oceanographer, but it also focuses on how he found the idea for his life by following his fascination with everything about sea life, cameras, and movies. "Movies fascinated Jacques, too. He wanted to know how they were made, how the cameras worked, and how chemicals made pictures appear on the film" (p. 7).

It's this fascination that every reader and writer has with certain topics that leads each of us to discover more, read more, write more, and wonder more. This is what we hope our students will learn over time in school: Good writing gives them a frisson of excitement that alerts the writer in them that there is more, much more, to find out about this idea. Ask students to talk about what fascinations they might have about things that occur in life or what they've noticed and are curious about. Let them know that it's possible to use those ideas as springboards for writing, regardless of the purpose—narrative, informational, or opinion.

. . . .

"Not Just Any Gum Tree" (sign)

written by the Zoological Society of San Diego, San Diego, CA
(See the Appendix for the reproducible.)

The people at the San Diego Zoo sure know how to write for their visitors. This sign is an example of how they take complex ideas about an animal's food and habitat and make it understandable to a layperson. I found it fascinating to learn that there so many species of eucalyptus, for example, and that koalas know which ones they can eat and which to stay away from because they're toxic.

Notice that this sign sets out to inform readers about one thing: why koalas are such picky eaters in spite of the various species of eucalyptus trees all around them. Student writers can look at big ideas such as "What do animals eat?" and use this text as a model for how to focus the topic to something much smaller and more manageable to research and use for writing. Brainstorm a list of big topics, such as sports, U.S. history, music, oceans, science fiction, and ceramic art. Have groups of students come up with a list of five or six smaller, more focused topics that could be the subject of further research and become ideas for writing. If any of the ideas sparks a frisson for students, encourage them to record it in their writer's notebook for future reference. Or, you could create a series of signs about the topics students choose, such as this everyday mentor text from the San Diego Zoo.

. . . .

> **Key Quality: Developing the Topic.** The writer provides enough critical evidence to support the theme and shows insight on the topic, or the writer tells the story in a fresh way through an original, unpredictable plot.

Moonbird: A Year on the Wind With the Great Survivor B95

written by Phillip Hoose

Farrar, Straus and Giroux, 2012

This award-winning account of a *rufa* red shorebird was named B95 by the scientists who studied him and his remarkable life. This little bird, quite ordinary in many ways, turned out to be quite extraordinary, traveling amazing distances between Tierra del Fuego (an archipelago south of South America) and the Canadian Artic every year for over 20 years. This book not only documents everything about B95's habits and patterns but also reveals how the *rufa* species is endangered due to human activities.

As a longer, more expansive text than a simple picture book or sign, I recommend finding a passage that illustrates what you are trying to show about the writing and what you hope a student is interested enough in that he or she asks you later to read the entire book. It also allows you to choose more complex materials as mentor texts because students aren't reading the whole book, but rather examining parts of it for a quality of writing. In this case, read aloud the Preface, which is short and powerful, and then show the Table of Contents and the topics for each chapter.

> Meet B95, one of the world's premier athletes. Weighing a mere four ounces, he's flown more than 325,000 miles in his life—the distance to the moon and nearly halfway back. He flies at mountaintop height along ancient routes that lead him to his breeding grounds and back. But changes throughout his migratory circuit are challenging this Superbird and threatening to wipe out his entire subspecies of *rufa* red knot. Places that are critical for B95 and his flock to rest and refuel—stepping-stones along a vast annual migration network—have been altered by human activity. Can these places and the food they contain be preserved?
>
> Or will B95's and *rufa*'s days of flight soon come to an end? (p. 3)

By reading about the main idea of the book in the Preface and pointing out how the idea is developed in each of the subsequent chapters, students learn that to develop an idea, their writing requires information and planning. They explore how the development of the idea stays on track from beginning to end. Have students look at science and social studies textbooks to see how the big idea of the book is broken down into chapters, and how chapters are broken down into subsections, so all the information from start to finish clearly develops the main idea.

. . . .

Key Quality: Using Details. The writer offers credible, accurate details that create pictures in the reader's mind, from the beginning of the piece to the end. Those details provide the reader with evidence of the writer's knowledge about and/or experience with the topic.

Poop: A Natural History of the Unmentionable

written by Nicola Davies, illustrated by Neal Layton
Candlewick, 2004

This book needs little explanation. In her signature, delightful style, Nicola Davies provides a tour of poop: what it's good for, why it looks different from species to species, and its role in the ecosystem. There's little question that the information in the book will fascinate student readers and writers—and make them giggle. Details such as biggest, smallest, highest (yes, highest), and smelliest got my attention, but here are details about fossil poop that I found intriguing as well:

> No one will ever see a Tyrannosaurus rex eating its dinner, but along with fossils of its skeleton, T. rex has left some fossil poop, called coprolites. Coprolites found with T. rex bones in Canada contained fragments of a triceratops's ribs. What's more, the ribs had tooth marks that matched T. rex teeth, showing that the big predators had slashed their teeth along the side of a triceratops, ripping flesh and bones. T. rex poop had shown not only what was for dinner 70 million years ago but also how it was eaten! (pp. 54–55)

Poop may not be the subject that you want students writing more about, but it certainly opens the door to other, similar science-related ideas on which students can write in detail, such as tears, sweat, and urine. Feel free to branch out to whatever topics this book inspires but make sure students understand that the secret to writing like Davies does is using details that are factual in an interesting way.

The Organization Trait and Informational Writing

Organization: The internal structure of the piece

Organization of informational text is how writers show readers order, connections, hierarchy, and importance of ideas in the writing. It's how readers follow the idea to make meaning. Organization begins with having a powerful lead to grab the reader's attention. It needs to say, "Listen to this. You're going to find it really interesting, and you'll come to think about this topic in a whole new way." It shouldn't be too cute, and it certainly shouldn't be predictable.

The body of informational text can be organized in a variety of ways, including point-by-point analysis, deductive logic, cause and effect, comparison and contrast, problem and solution, and order of importance and complexity. Chronological structure may also be applied to informational writing. The informational writer has many choices to organize the body of the text to make his or her ideas stand out.

The end of an informational piece wraps up the thinking, draws conclusions, and leaves the reader with a bigger picture of the topic than when he or she began reading. Endings are tough; getting the right sense of closure is a lot more difficult than, "Thank you for reading my report," "The end," or "Now you know why bubble gum is not welcome in most schools."

The key to success in the organization trait is logic: fitting information together by thinking about what makes sense first, second, and last. Writers should build to a high point, placing the key piece of information at the "just right" place. It's writing, so there's no magic formula; it's an art as much as a science. Whatever you do, don't fall for formulas as the cure-all for organization. They produce deadly boring prose and take all the thinking out of the hands of the writer.

Mentor Texts and the Organization Trait

Key Quality: Creating the Lead. The writer grabs the reader's attention from the start and leads him or her into the piece naturally. The writer entices the reader, providing a tantalizing glimpse of what's to come.

Noah Webster & His Words

written by Jeri Chase Ferris, illustrated by Vincent X. Kirsch
Houghton Mifflin Harcourt, 2012

"Noah Webster always knew he was right, and he never got tired of saying so (even if, sometimes, he wasn't). He was, he said, 'full of CON-FI-DENCE' [noun: belief that one is right] from the very beginning." What a lead! Not only does it grab my attention with its form, but it also gives the reader all the clues needed to understand that Noah Webster is the dictionary guy. It's a perfect way to begin this biographical account of Webster's life.

To use this book as a mentor text for creating a lead, gather a group of biographies—picture books and chapter books—and inspect them for their beginning lines or opening paragraph. Ask students to categorize each, such as (a) a biographical item about the subject, (b) the setting where the subject grew up, (c) a little known fact, or (d) a clever way to introduce why the subject is famous. Ask students to explain to one another which they find the most effective and explain why. Encourage them to use that same technique on a piece of their own informational writing that's currently in process.

· ·

"Here, Kitty Kitty: Monopoly Rolls Out Its New Token" (online article)

written by Chris Morris
Plugged In, 2013

In a bold move, the makers of the classic board game Monopoly held a worldwide contest and replaced one of the traditional game pieces with the players' choice: out with the iron and in with the cat. This online article explains the contest and the outcome. Short, fact-filled paragraphs accent the use of sequence and transition words and phrases, such as *nearly, finally, in addition, given the fact*, and *as for the iron.*

Ask students to explain the difference between a sequence word (time/order sequence) and transition words (connect ideas and show relationships). Look for examples of each in this mentor text and have students continue to add to both lists from additional texts that they consult as well. Discuss the locations of sequence and transition words in sentences and how the words can be embedded into a sentence, not just placed at the beginning, and why this might be a good writing technique.

. . . .

> **Key Quality: Developing the Body.** The writer creates a piece that's easy to follow by fitting details together logically. The writer slows down to spotlight important points or events and speeds up when he or she needs to move the reader along.

Locomotive

written and illustrated by Brian Floca
Atheneum Books for Young Readers, 2013

The impact of the Transcontinental Railroad on travel across the United States back in 1869 is lusciously illustrated and lyrically described in this 2014 Caldecott Medal winner. It's filled with examples of organizational structures, from the inside cover pages that highlight the railroad's map route from east to west, to the end pages that explain how steam power works. The core information on the pages, however, chronicles the journey of family and crew on the newly built railroad line as they stop in one location after the next, exploring the different regions of the country.

Have students make a route map of the story as you travel together through the pages of this magnificent book. As you read and discuss, ask them to write about favorite places described in the book and key them to a U.S. map. Put all the descriptions together in one class book in the order that they appeared in the story, making sure students use the U.S. map as a check for which would come first, next, and last. Make a cover and share the class book with other students by placing it in the library next to the original text.

. . . .

On a Beam of Light: A Story of Albert Einstein

written by Jennifer Berne, illustrated by Vladimir Radunsky
Chronicle, 2013

Albert Einstein, one of the most famous and influential scientists of all time, didn't speak until he was 3, but once he began, he drove everyone crazy by asking questions—important questions. And he kept asking them until the day he died. The text is lyrical; it flows elegantly from page to page. The big idea is powerful: that endless wondering about life can lead to profound understandings. Take a close look at the ending because it sums this picture book up perfectly. Einstein's thinking helped us figure out things about time and space that no one had ever considered before, but his wonderings also leave us with more big questions to answer now and in the future. The book supplies endnotes with even more fascinating tidbits about Einstein. This is what the key quality is all about: closure and taking the idea to a bigger place in the reader's mind.

Coming up with an ending is one of the hardest parts of writing. But guess what? The best way to teach this key quality is right at your fingertips—within the covers of the coveted books that are already in your collections. Send students to your classroom or school library and ask them to find an ending that they think works well in a book and write it out. I call this a scavenger hunt, and I use this strategy often for many different key qualities of writing. Have a student read the ending and ask the rest of the class to figure out what book it comes from or guess what the book might be about. Encourage students to talk about what the writer did in the ending that worked well—well enough that the student stole it as a mentor text.

The Voice Trait and Informational Writing

Voice: The tone and tenor of the piece

Voice is the quality of writing that connects the reader and the writer. When a writer is excited about the topic of informational writing, it shows itself through the conviction, authority, credibility, and authenticity of how the ideas are presented. To create voice, writers should come across to the reader as knowledgeable and trustworthy. Readers should not doubt the authenticity of facts, figures, or information. They should have no doubt that the writer has given them the right information.

Writing is a thinking skill, and as such, there isn't a single right way to construct text to achieve voice. Every time a writer sits down to write, a complicated matrix of writing skills must be applied. Decisions about the idea, organization, voice, word choice, sentence fluency, and conventions are made and carried out—sometimes successfully, sometimes not. Voice shows up when the different traits are working well in the writing; it's a primary trait. When the other traits of writing are handled expertly, the authenticity of the voice surfaces and is recognized by the writer. Voice is not a matter of being correct; rather, it's a matter of connecting to the reader.

The key to success in voice is when writers exude confidence about the topic and feel free to express themselves in new and original ways, always staying true to the facts and information presented.

Mentor Texts and the Voice Trait

Key Quality: Establishing a Tone. The writer cares about the topic, and it shows. The writing is expressive and compelling. The reader feels the writer's conviction, authority, and integrity.

The Beginner's Guide to Running Away From Home
written by Jennifer LaRue Huget, illustrated by Red Nose Studio
Schwartz & Wade, 2013

This "how-to" book is sure to bring a smile. Having been wronged by a baby brother, a baby sister, and his parents, the main character's voice takes on a petulant tone as he explains why he's running away and his plans for doing it. The writing seems so authentic that you can almost hear his whining and complaining out loud. He knows his options and considers them carefully, step by step, eventually discarding them all, of course, and making his peace with the idea of going home and staying there.

This hilarious book is a good launching pad for both tone and the how-to format (organization). Ask students to identify words that describe the tone in this book compared with the tone of most how-to books that they might know or that you provide. They will likely be much different. Then, ask students to work with a partner to come up with the topic for another how-to text with a distinctive tone like Huget's and share ideas.

Clemente!

written by Willie Perdomo, illustrated by Bryan Collier
Henry Holt, 2010

A young boy asks his father why he was named Clemente in this poignant retelling of Robert Clemente's life. As the father explains, we learn about the passion and commitment that Clemente had for the game of baseball and for the needs of others, especially the victims of the 1972 earthquake in Nicaragua. Clemente's life was cut short when he was flying to bring first aid and supplies and his plane crashed into the sea. Through English and Spanish words throughout the text—adding another level of authenticity—we learn that Clemente braved racism and terrible adversity but never gave up. This spirit of determination is why the young boy in the story was named after this famous baseball player.

The purpose of this book is to introduce the reader to a person whose life is worth remembering and emulating. The author accomplishes that by using voice to help readers relate to Clemente's life. Ask students who, in today's world, might be remembered for their good works, and discuss the voice they'd use in those biographies.

. . . .

"Please Be Safe" (sign)
(See the Appendix for the reproducible.)

Sometimes changing the point of view can be the delightful surprise that hooks the reader. This sign explains the consequences for the animal, not the human, which makes it stand out from other signs, more traditionally worded as, "Be careful," "Do not climb," or "Danger." This is a sign that the intended audience will read and feel a connection to. And hopefully, they'll indeed be safe and careful around the fence.

Give students a few days to notice safety signs around the school or in their neighborhoods and compare the voice in those with the one in this sign. Ask students to revise a sign that has no voice to one that has lots of voice, such as this "Please Be Safe" example, so it connects to the intended audience.

. . . .

Bugs in My Hair!
written and illustrated by David Shannon
Blue Sky, 2013

Ewww. It's one of those topics that no one wants to talk about but that every school has to deal with: head lice. In this highly energized picture book, Shannon explains lice, where they come from, how it feels to have them, and what to do if you get them. It's a very risky topic, but he handles it expertly, and as always, his illustrations make the pages come to life.

It would be equally risky (but fun!) to have students take on the point of view of the lice and write about their life cycle. More research would need to take place, of course, but finding information and then putting it into this lively format might be just the recipe for voice-filled writing of their own.

The Word Choice Trait and Informational Writing

Word choice: The vocabulary the writer uses to convey meaning and enlighten the reader

The way the writer uses accurate and specific words is critical in informational writing. Readers expect to see words that inform and explain the subject area, which, in turn, lend credibility to how much the writer knows about the topic. But the other key qualities in word choice matter greatly, too. For informational writing to reach the status of "literature," we expect to see figurative language as well as other words that capture our imaginations. We yearn for finely honed words and phrases that explain and inform, not just the first wording that came to the writer's mind. And, of course, the verbs are critical in any kind of writing—narrative, informational, or argument. They power the sentences.

The key to success in word choice is to develop the writer's vocabulary in every discipline and in the English language across the board. You can never fill up a writer's word bank. The curiosity we develop in students about words and how to use them well will support them for a lifetime.

A man with a scant vocabulary will almost certainly be a weak thinker. The richer and more copious one's vocabulary and the greater one's awareness of fine distinctions and subtle nuances of meaning, the more fertile and precise is likely to be one's thinking. Knowledge of things and knowledge of the words for them grow together. If you do not know the words, you can hardly know the thing. (Hazlitt, 1993, p. 51)

Mentor Texts and the Word Choice Trait

Key Quality: Using Strong Verbs. The writer uses many action words, giving the piece punch and pizzazz. The writer has stretched to find lively verbs that add energy to the piece.

Older Than the Stars

written by Karen C. Fox, illustrated by Nancy Davis
Charlesbridge, 2010

> Each star shone brightly for billions of years. But stars don't live forever. Whenever a star died, it exploded in a giant fireball called a supernova. The searing heat of the supernova forced some of the star's atoms to melt together into new metals like iron, copper, and gold. The explosion sent all the atoms—big and small—hurtling through the universe in all directions.

Shone, died, exploded, forced, melt—these verbs and more come from just this one passage. Every page of this informational and artistically formatted book demonstrates how to use strong verbs. It's a simple and beautiful treatment of the theoretical model of the big bang theory and how the universe was formed.

After a quick review of the role of verbs in sentences, show students this text, page by page, and pluck out the verbs from each line, noting how many are active verbs and which they feel are the most powerful.

. . . .

Ocean Sunlight: How Tiny Plants Feed the Seas

written by Molly Bang and Penny Chisholm, illustrated by Molly Bang
Blue Sky, 2012

Ocean Sunlight gives us page after page of beautiful words and phrases as Bang and Chisholm explain the sun's light and how it provides what the ocean's living things—plants and animals—need to exist. Passages such as "The deep cold waters underneath are pitch black dark—darker than the darkest, moonless, starless night" are stellar examples of the richness of the language in this beautifully written and illustrated picture book.

Ask students which images are the most powerful in this text, and go back and read those passages again, noting what Bang and Chisholm have done with words to create such vivid imagery. Students may wish to create their own illustrations of this visual writing that go with additional passages from the text.

· · · · · · · · · · · · · · · · · · · ·

"Dr. Marla R. Emery, Geographer" (card)

written by the USDA Forest Service
(See the Appendix for the reproducible, as well as the URL for the card in color.)

In the USDA Forest Service's Scientists' Card series, students can read about and discover many different jobs related to science and "meet" individual scientists who have those positions. These cards are two sided, like baseball trading cards—very cool! Each card contains a great deal of specific and accurate information about the particular science profession, along with interests of the highlighted scientist and how he or she got into that field of work.

Students may want to design similar cards for historical figures, book characters, famous athletes, as so on. Ask them to take care to use language that explains their skills and the types of jobs they have with great care—choosing the "just right" words to create details that are both specific and accurate.

. . . .

> **Key Quality: Using Language Effectively.** The writer uses words to capture the reader's imagination and enhance the piece's meaning. There's a deliberate attempt to choose the best word over the first word that comes to mind.

Eight Days Gone

written by Linda McReynolds, illustrated by Ryan O'Rourke
Charlesbridge, 2012

Sometimes less is more in word choice, and this "not as simple as it looks" rhyming picture book about *Apollo 11* and the first moon landing is an excellent example. The author is a poet, so not surprisingly, she packs a lot of punch in each carefully selected word:

> Desolation.
> Silent. Dark.
> Tranquil sea.
> Barren. Stark.

You don't have to go to the moon to understand, in these seven words, just how bleak it is on the surface.

The right, carefully chosen language creates understanding. Encourage students to pick a topic, such as the first snowfall or the hottest day of the year, and describe it factually but poetically, using words carefully and effectively to create meaning.

The Sentence Fluency Trait and Informational Writing

Sentence fluency: The way words and phrases flow through the piece

Think about this trait as a twofer. It not only covers the correct grammatical construction of sentences but also includes how they sound—how those correctly formed sentences flow across the page. It's a visual *and* auditory trait. When we teach students to write correct sentences, we focus on simple, compound, and complex sentence patterns and the rules for each. When we teach students to write sentences that sound smooth, we read aloud, note what the author has done to make the passage fluent, and show them how to accomplish the same fluency in their own writing. To master both of these parts of sentence fluency requires two different sets of skills.

In informational writing, a writer is usually aware of the audience and the readers' reading level. When writing to elementary-age students, for instance, a writer will simplify sentence structure to make sure readers are reading at or slightly above what's comfortable for them. To write sentences too far above the heads of student writers would make reading informational text painfully hard and frustrating, leading to a total turnoff. At the same time, to write sentences that are all too simply constructed would bore the reader.

The key to success in sentence fluency is learning how to listen to writing right along with reading it with your eyes. Helping students hear how writing should sound makes all the difference when they write their own texts.

Mentor Texts and the Sentence Fluency Trait

Key Quality: Capturing Smooth and Rhythmic Flow. The writer thinks about how the sentences sound. The writer uses phrasing that is almost musical. If the piece were read aloud, it would be easy on the ear.

Team Moon: How 400,000 People Landed Apollo 11 *on the Moon*
written by Catherine Thimmesh
Houghton Mifflin, 2006

This award-winning picture book with extended text tells the dramatic account of how the *Apollo 11* moon landing was planned and carried out. It's told through facts, information, and insiders' stories. I was particularly struck with the fluency in the piece in each of its many formats: quotes, stories, fact boxes, pictures, lists of challenges, and running text.

There are examples throughout of how the author creates smooth and rhythmic flow. For example, there are places where dashes are used to create a sense of urgency because of a problem that was occurring with the alarm system. Then, as seen in this example, Thimmesh uses single words and alliteration to keep the pace moving and underscore the urgency of the situation:

> Bales scoured his guidance and navigation data.
>> Searching. Sifting. Sorting.
>> Flight Director Kranz plucked details from a flood of incoming information.
>> Juggling. Judging. (p. 19)

This passage reads smoothly, but it takes a second look to understand why: The author makes it easy for us to hear the text as we read it.

Look for more examples of how authors use fluency to add interest to the writing in other books and everyday texts. Contrast this book with *Eight Days Gone* by Linda McReynolds for smooth and rhythmic flow. They may be on the same topic, but they're written in two completely different sentence styles.

· · · · · · · · · · · · · · · · · · ·

Cave Detectives:
Unraveling the Mystery of an Ice Age Cave
written by David L. Harrison, illustrated by Ashley Mims, photographs by Edward Biamonte
Chronicle, 2007

> A short-faced bear moves along a stream. He is a giant compared to any other bear that will ever live. He is mostly a carnivore, a meat eater. Whether he brings down his own prey, steals from smaller predators, or chases buzzards off a carcass, he is always hungry for meat. (p. 7)

So begins the first passage of Harrison's book. Each paragraph can be pulled and examined for sentence fluency. You won't be disappointed by the sentences you find, regardless of the page you turn to. Every page is rich with models of artfully crafted sentences. Harrison obviously knows his way around the sentence fluency trait. It's not surprising since Harrison is a poet as well, which might explain the lyrical nature of his prose.

Give books like this one to teams of students and ask them to find different types of sentences as you call them out: simple, compound, complex. Make it a contest to see who can find great examples the fastest, and talk about the teams' choices as they're selected.

. . . .

"Angry Birds Go! Jenga Pirate Pig Attack Game"
(product description)

written by Hasbro

(See the References section for the URL.)

"Arr, matey! The popular Angry Birds app comes to life in this epic Pirate Pig Attack Game! Can you triumph in this fast-crashing game?" (para. 1) begins the product description for this game from Hasbro. The text itemizes what's included with the game and includes a bulleted list of the game's features, too. Every type of sentence is modeled in this everyday text, and it has terrific voice—an added bonus.

Taking a closer look at how this product description is written, students will notice different sentence types and lengths, as well as the use of fragments. Challenge students to write up a similar product description that shows the range of sentence types for a favorite game or one they make up with a partner.

. . . .

Lifetime: The Amazing Numbers in Animal Lives
written by Lola M. Schaefer, illustrated by Christopher Silas Neal
Chronicle, 2013

Schaefer provides a variety of examples about how to use sentences in creative ways in this nonfiction text. She begins with a Preface about the book's intention, using traditional sentences that flow smoothly. But as she gets into the core of this picture book, she uses fragments and one-word sentences to punctuate her message. The text has a musical quality from beginning to end. In endnotes, Schaefer provides additional background and information on the animals spotlighted in the text, using complete sentences that are finely crafted and smooth sounding.

Once students have enjoyed this fascinating book of numerically ordered facts about animals, invite them to pick another animal and find an interesting fact about it that includes a number and could become a new page in this book that shows some risk taking or "rule" breaking with the sentences. Have them write out the more specific endnotes that go with their facts as well.

The Conventions Trait and Informational Writing

Conventions: The mechanical correctness of the piece

Conventions is the editing trait. It's where writers check the piece to make sure it's easy for readers to read. Many readers (not teachers—teachers can read anything!) won't stick with reading if there are problems with spelling, capitalization, punctuation, and grammar and usage. Or if they struggle through because it's business related, for example, they come away with a bad taste in their mouths about the writer's ability to communicate clearly.

There's no difference in how conventions are applied across the modes—informational, narrative, and argument writing. Writers need to use conventions well regardless of the purpose for writing. There will likely be dialogue that needs capitalization and punctuation in narrative writing, and there may be bulleted lists that require parallel construction in informational writing. Regardless, the rules are the same for all forms of writing. Readers can assume that mentor texts are published works and will be well edited, so the goal of using them to teach writing will be to showcase interesting things about the different conventions and to challenge students to show a range of skills with increasing complexity in conventions in their own writing.

The key to success in conventions is having grade-level expectations that are consistently reinforced. Making sure that students develop more sophisticated uses of conventions that build strategically, one year on the next, and making sure students handle the basics of conventions while being taught new information about each convention in every grade will help all young writers move forward in this critical trait.

Mentor Texts and the Conventions Trait

Key Quality: Checking Spelling. The writer spells sight words, high-frequency words, and less familiar words correctly. When the writer spells less familiar words incorrectly, those words are phonetically correct. Overall, the piece reveals control in spelling.

Dear Deer: A Book of Homophones
written and illustrated by Gene Barretta
Henry Holt, 2007

There are no trickier spelling issues to conquer than the dreaded homophones. This picture book addresses words that sound alike and are spelled differently. It's a refreshing way for students to revisit these spelling demons. The addition of a picture may help them visualize a word, its spelling, and its meaning better than just trying to memorize the word. In all likelihood, students have been fussing with homophones for years, so taking a new approach may be just what they need to master these types of words.

Students might enjoy trying their hands at writing sentences that use homophones and illustrating them, as is done in this picture book. It may be a challenge for them to come up with a sentence that uses *to, two,* and *too* in it, for instance, but it'll certainly make them think about the differences among these words in meaning and spelling.

. . . .

Key Quality: Using Punctuation and Indenting Paragraphs. The writer handles basic punctuation skillfully. The writer understands how to use periods, commas, question marks, and exclamation points to enhance clarity and meaning. Paragraphs are indented in the right places. The piece is ready for a general audience.

Eats, Shoots & Leaves:
Why Commas Really Do Make a Difference!
written by Lynne Truss, illustrated by Bonnie Timmons
G.P. Putnam's Sons, 2006

Hilarious is the only word to describe this picture book on punctuation that grows out of the original text targeted for adults by the same author. Truss shows quite clearly why punctuation can change the meaning of what you write, beginning with the joke in the title. Is it, What does the panda eat? (shoots and leaves), or, What does the panda do? (eats, shoots, and leaves)? Clearly, in the second version, there's a killer panda on the loose. Yikes! And it's all because of punctuation.

Sharing the examples in this picture book should inspire students to come up with their own sentences that change meaning based on punctuation only. Try this one: "Student without her teacher is nothing," versus, "Student, without her, teacher is nothing."

. . . .

M.O.M. (Mom Operating Manual)
written by Doreen Cronin, illustrated by Laura Cornell
Atheneum Books for Young Readers, 2011

Because the title of this book is an acronym, it can be a great resource to help students understand what acronyms are and how to capitalize them. Of course, the book is also filled with good examples of capitalization handled well in proper nouns, titles, and headings.

Ask students to come up with different book ideas that could be turned into acronym titles, and let them write the title pages and illustrate them. Show students how to capitalize subtitles, the author's name, the publisher, and other proper nouns, such as cities and states.

. . . .

"School Kids Correct Celebrity Grammar Mistakes on Twitter" (blog post)
written by Lauren O'Neil
Your Community Blog, 2013

Vedic19
@DanielRadcliffe
Hello guys ,It have been an age that I didn't tweet , thanks all for your amaizing messages .DAN XX

Red Balloon
@redballoonBR
DanielRadcliffe Dear Harry Potter, I'm Gabriel, from Brazil. Your tweet has 2 mistakes: "it has been" and "amazing". (para. 4)

This blog discusses the way 8–13-year-old Brazilian students at their school, Red Balloon, have used Twitter to follow famous people and scrutinize their messages for grammar mistakes. I can't think of a better way to drive home the point that grammar matters, no matter what the medium.

Gather some age-appropriate tweets from sources you trust, such as public television or Nickelodeon, identify grammar problems, solve them together, and then write back. Of course, it's important to make sure the tweets are appropriate. This is a very savvy way for students to use their knowledge about grammar in a real context. It's fun, it's fast, and it's learning in action.

Ask students to generate a list of rules for a resource that they can keep adding to that shows how they corrected the grammar in the tweets they've been given. Ask students to write out the rules that they applied in a lively and engaging voice so others can enjoy using the resource during the year to make sure the grammar in their writing is correct, too.

The Presentation Trait and Informational Writing

Presentation: The physical appearance of the piece

Presentation is the +1 trait that really isn't a true writing trait but rather more of a feature of writing. By the time writing is ready to share, it's important for it to have a clean, clear appearance that the reader finds inviting—whether it's handwritten or word processed. Presentation is more of a fine motor and visual skill than a pure writing skill.

However, in informational writing, the impact of presentation is made not only by having neat writing or using a wise choice of font and size but also by including the use of easy-to-find headings, bullets, page numbers, charts, maps, graphs, and tables. They help by making the information accessible for the reader. Presentation may actually play a larger role in informational writing, therefore, than in the other modes. Regardless, presentation matters to readers and gives them an impression of the writing before a single word is read.

The key to success in this trait is readability. Think of presentation as the welcome mat that invites the reader into the text.

Mentor Texts and the Presentation Trait

Dr. Amelia's Boredom Survival Guide:
First Aid for Rainy Days, Boring Errands,
Waiting Rooms, Whatever!
written and illustrated by Marissa Moss
Simon & Schuster Books for Young Readers, 2006

The Amelia series has many titles, but I like the how-to ones the best. This one is clever and imaginative but still provides lots of useful information for the bored kid who doesn't know how to make use of time that isn't scheduled, is dragged along on errands, or flat-out doesn't know what to do to entertain him- or herself. The books are formatted to appear that they are handwritten journals with drawings and photos. The "handwriting" is a font, of course, but it could be a good jumping-off place to discuss the use of fonts in word processing.

Ask students what catches their eye on the pages of this book and then talk about each element. Create a list of things that matter for strong presentation in writing, whether handwritten or word processed. Have students write new pages for this survival guide to boredom on topics of their choice, using the different text features that they decided were important.

. . . .

Girls Think of Everything:
Stories of Ingenious Inventions by Women
written by Catherine Thimmesh, illustrated by Melissa Sweet
Houghton Mifflin, 2000

The way this book flows, using one font in the running text broken only by italics to lighten the text-heavy pages, works well. And the use of a bold pink (the book is about girls, of course) in a second font for boxed information on every page is very eye appealing. This is a style that students could copy quite easily. It allows for a lot of information on every page, but it breaks up the word-processed text with shape and color.

Ask students to consider how many fonts work well on a page. As they look at different books and resource materials, have students keep track of the number of fonts and font sizes for the ones they think are the most readable. Many graphic designers recommend one or two fonts on a word-processed page, but other book designers go wild with fonts. Focus the discussions on readability and see what guidelines students feel work best for their word-processed texts.

. . . .

Oh My Gods! A Look-It-Up Guide
to the Gods of Mythology (Mythlopedia)
written by Megan E. Bryant
Scholastic, 2010

This is one of my all-time favorite books. It's an encyclopedia (mythlopedia) of the Greek gods and goddesses and their families. The content is presented in a graphic novel style: part drawing, part pictures, part text, part lots of things. The layout is busy, which makes it an interesting piece to examine for the use of white space. Even though there isn't very much of it on individual pages, it's used strategically so each deliciously cluttered page draws your eye to the different columns and sections.

Students love this book (and so do I), which is the first of a four-part series. Invite them to explain what it is about the way each page is laid out that attracts the eye and have a thoughtful discussion of the use and abuse of white space in writing. Ask students to create guidelines for using white space in handwritten and word-processed text that would apply with and without illustrations.

. . . .

Key Quality: *Incorporating Text Features.* The writer effectively places text features, such as titles, headings, page numbers, and bullets, on the page and aligns them clearly with the text they support.

everyday ET text "Kid-Friendly Fun, Rain or Shine!" (brochure)
written by the Susquehanna River Valley Visitor's Bureau
(See the Appendix for the reproducible of the brochure's front cover only, as well as the URL for the entire brochure in color.)

This brochure of kid-friendly attractions in the Susquehanna River Valley in Pennsylvania is a fine example of how to use creative text features, such as styling words in the shapes they describe (e.g., *rain, shine*), along with using colorful headings for the different types of places: "Yummy Treats," "Movie Theaters," "Miniature Golf & Batting Cages" (p. 1), and so on. These folks have thought about how to make the brochure kid friendly while appealing to adults as well.

Using this brochure as a model, have the class design a brochure for your own town and the many different recreational opportunities it offers. Encourage students to have fun with drawing the words right along with writing them by designing the brochure so it shows different text features that make it easy and enjoyable to read.

Wrapping Up Informational Writing

Students will likely find that informational writing is what they'll do most often in their lives within and outside of school. Writing strong informational pieces is a key to college and career readiness as well.

Models of informational writing are everywhere—short, long, and everything in between. Informational writing is everywhere. It's the easiest type of writing to find in the everyday world and one of the most fun types to collect if you're a writing thief. Narrative writing, on the other hand, makes rare appearances in the everyday world. It exists, but you have to really look to find it. But search we must because narrative writing is essential to learn as well. Narrative writing teaches us about life, loss, love, and our humanity. It pulls at our heartstrings; it allows us glimpses inside people's lives that we'd never understand otherwise. It entertains. It makes us feel. Stories are a very powerful way that we communicate important ideas. In Chapter 4, we'll discuss narrative writing and the mentor texts that you can use to teach it as you focus on each of the traits and their key qualities.

CHAPTER 4

Narrative Writing

I grew up a fiction lover. Reading was an essential survival skill for my gypsy lifestyle that landed me in a different town, or a different part of town, every six months or so. I didn't invest in good friends because I was just going to move again soon anyway, so I gathered virtual friends through books. I felt connected to the characters in books who were always there for me, day or night, regardless of my zip code. What better way to come to understand the depth of friendship than through E.B. White's *Charlotte's Web*, which I read many times, crying at the end every time. I wanted to travel to Oz to visit friends I'd made in L. Frank Baum's books by reading the whole series again and again. I'd stand by the grandfather clock in the hallway midday on Saturday, like Dorothy did, and click my heels together, dreaming that I could go to that magical land, far, far away from my everyday life. Stories and the characters and places in them became an extension of my life—a secret cache of friends I could draw on whenever I felt the need.

I've never outgrown my deep and lasting love of story. I'll do almost anything to steal time to read a good one. I've actually told my editor (shhh…) that there was no Wi-Fi on the plane while traveling to a workshop far from my home in Portland, Oregon, just so I could fall into a novel instead of writing and revising for a deadline. Truthfully, there are times when I actually bemoan the wheels touching down, forcing me to stop reading.

As I've thought about the impact of story on my life and on young readers everywhere, I've struggled a bit with the language we use to talk about this mode and its genres. *Story, narrative, fiction, nonfiction*—these terms tend to blur in educational literature, so it seems useful to clarify them. Here's my understanding:

- *Narrative:* The structure of fiction or nonfiction events—the architectural design of the story or series of stories that are often open ended, such as the story of the presidency

- *Story:* The sequence of events (beginning, middle, and end) that includes characters, setting, plot, problem, and resolution, such as the story of my son Sam's first time driving with a stick shift
- *Fiction narratives:* Stories that come from the imagination, such as realistic fiction, science fiction, fantasy, tall tales, and dystopia
- *Nonfiction narratives:* Stories that are based on facts, such as memoirs, biographies, autobiographies, and diaries

Another murky area in narrative writing is our understanding of the difference between facts and truth. Some people feel that facts alone make pieces "true." But facts are just facts. The reader interprets their importance and validity based on how they're used in the story. There will be facts in fiction as well as nonfiction. Truth is a bigger issue. I love this distinction between facts and truth by Madeline L'Engle: "'Truth is what is true, and it's not necessarily factual....Truth and fact are not the same thing. Truth does not contradict or deny facts, but it goes through and beyond facts'" (Rosenberg, 2006, p. 69). I believe that authors of all stories, whether nonfiction or fiction, seek to find the truth by using facts, and I think that's one of the many reasons we're drawn to them.

Think about what you enjoy reading across all genres (realistic fiction, science fiction, fantasy, fairy tales, tall tales, and so on). What's the common thread? Narrative. How the story is told; how truth is revealed. Children are drawn to narrative writing. In fact, I don't remember reading anything nonfiction for pleasure until I was much older than my child self. I didn't read anything "real" unless it was assigned in school in a content area (or in a fan magazine about the Beatles), and my English classes were dominated by fiction. I simply wasn't interested in biographies or memoirs, although now I find both quite enjoyable, especially memoir. I'm a big fan of this genre, likely because its narrative structure is familiar landscape for me as a reader. For me, memoir is that perfect blend of fiction and nonfiction. It's story, but it's about someone real, it's factually accurate, and it seeks the truth of this person's life. In a well-written memoir, the best qualities of fiction have been stolen and worked into nonfiction, satisfying my thirst for story.

Good writing is always about telling a story, regardless of how that story is conveyed. Informational and argument writing tell stories— just in a different way. They don't employ a plotline, characters, or a problem to be resolved, but rather, these texts tell the story of what we need to know, why the information is important, what matters, and why we should care. And often, to accomplish all of this, these texts include anecdotes and stories to make key points clear and show their importance. Argument takes it up a notch and establishes a position by inserting a claim and a counterclaim about the information. Many of the best-written argument pieces use narrative techniques as the architecture or design to show importance, order, and emphasis. Stories can be part of how the writer supports the argument. The writer uses stories judiciously as evidence, applying reason and logic that connect ideas to the reader's experience, which in turn contributes to their validity.

Fiction and Nonfiction Matters

The books and materials used to teach in English/language arts classes have changed since I was a young person long ago—and for the better. No longer can a student go through 13 years of education and not read and come to appreciate the fine nonfiction that exists in the classroom, libraries, and the world. This shift is evident as the Common Core State Standards ramp up the emphasis on nonfiction to a whole new level, gradually over the K–12 years, until about 70% of the recommended reading for high school students is nonfiction.

My reaction to this emphasis on reading nonfiction is complicated by my own reading taste and how much I believe story adds to the lives of students. Yet, I fully recognize the need for more high-quality nonfiction in every classroom. The recommended proportion of nonfiction and fiction reading may well mirror the reading we do in our everyday lives, but I believe school should be more than a training ground for college and the workplace. It should prepare students for life, the kind of life they find between the pages of fiction texts as they pose questions of ethics, responsibility, moral dilemmas, integrity, and honor. The bottom line is that I completely support the inclusion of more nonfiction reading and writing in every class, but not at the expense of fiction.

Fiction is the thinker's laboratory—the place where life is explored and considered. It allows us to feel love and loss and sort out everything in between. Through fiction, we sample the complexity of life and how it feels when it's unfair or unjust in the real and imagined worlds. We find out why friends are important. We live in families, cultures, and civilizations that are different from our own. I recently finished reading a fascinating literary fable: *Mr. Penumbra's 24-Hour Bookstore,* a novel by Robin Sloan (2012). In it, the author makes the case that books "are like open cities, with all sorts of ways to wander in" (p. 180). Rather than setting percentages and numbers, I believe our aim for reading should include big doses of fiction and nonfiction so readers meander through every kind of text to fully explore and pilfer its riches.

> **❝ It's more than story; good fiction teaches, too. ❞**

As my younger self came to know, fiction is a key ingredient in every reader's diet. It's more than story; good fiction teaches, too. Growing up in Los Angeles, I would never have lived on a farm such as the one in *Charlotte's Web,* but I gained an insider's knowledge about one from E.B. White. I didn't ride in a wagon to settle in a new, wild country, but I could appreciate the hardships that were endured and the love that the family had for one another in *Little House on the Prairie* by Laura Ingalls Wilder. I was a different person as I closed the cover of each of these powerful books, more educated and more informed.

Fiction continues to teach and coax and challenge me today. It's why I continue reading *To Kill a Mockingbird* each summer and why I eagerly awaited the arrival of *The Hunger Games: Catching Fire* movie—so I could be caught up in that mind space once again. It's why a nation of viewers, including me, binge-watch great stories in series television, such as *Breaking Bad, The Borgias,* and *Downton Abbey.* Binge-watching television satisfies that need to be caught up and swept away by the magic of a story that's well told over an extended period of time—much like reading a great book.

The Power of Narrative

Whether true, made up, or a combination of both, narrative is an effective method for exploring any topic. Whether it presents as realistic fiction, science fiction, fantasy, history, memoir, or biography, narratives develop by using time as the key organizational feature. And whether they're crafting fiction or nonfiction, writers employ many of the same narrative devices, such as flashback, flash forward, and circular patterns, to develop their stories—stories that are a powerful means of explaining and entertaining. Even William Zinsser (2006), the model of clear, informational writing, admits, "the novelist can take us into hidden places where no other writer can go: into the deep emotions and the interior life" (p. 99).

Good Writing Tells a Story, Period

So, how is narrative writing different from the informational writing that we just explored in the last chapter? The answer appears to be obvious: Narrative writing tells a story, whereas informational writing explains and describes. But good writing can do both—tell a story to relate information, or share new information as a story. The difference between the two is the primary purpose for the writing. When all is said and done, when the last page is turned, when you turn off your e-reader or click off a website, you aren't thinking about purpose; you're only thinking about your engagement with the reading: if you're caught up in the idea, if it answered your questions, if it brought you to a new way of thinking, or if it piqued your curiosity and, if so, how quickly you can get back to it. And it might be a combination of several, if not all, of the above. The finest texts tend to steal liberally from aspects of all the modes to make the primary purpose clear.

In fact, narratives can serve many purposes, but without fail, good narratives entertain and teach. In *Where the Red Fern Grows* by Wilson Rawls, the writer's voice draws you into every line on every page, and when you read, you feel like you're experiencing the story right along with the characters. But Rawls does more than just tell a great story. When we read this classic, we understand poverty and strength, heartache and loss. We learn what respect and loyalty look like in the most difficult of circumstances. The primary purpose of this magnificent book is to tell a story: a narrative. But I believe the effect of the purpose goes much deeper. *Where the Red Fern Grows* satisfies, entertains, saddens, challenges, and teaches. The stories we love and that stand the test of time manage to do it all.

It's difficult to create a hard-and-fast definition of the narrative modes because of this inherent complexity of the multiple purposes for which we write. The truth is, good writers mix modes to create the text they want. Look at these examples pulled from *Harry Potter and the Sorcerer's Stone* by J.K. Rowling (1999), an iconic narrative text:

"This," said Wood, "is the Golden Snitch, and it's the most important ball of the lot. It's very hard to catch because it's so fast and difficult to see. It's the Seeker's job to catch it. You've got to weave in and out of the Chasers, Beaters, Bludgers, and Quaffle to get it before the other team's Seeker, because whichever Seeker catches the Snitch wins his team an extra hundred and fifty points, so they nearly always win....A game of Quidditch only ends when the Snitch is caught, so it can go on for ages. (p. 169)

Harry left the locker room alone some time later, to take his Nimbus Two Thousand back to the broomshed. He couldn't ever remember feeling happier. He'd really done something to be proud of now—no one could say he was just a famous name any more. The evening air had never smelled so sweet. He walked over the damp grass, reliving the last hour in his head, which was a happy blur: Gryffindors running to lift him onto their shoulders; Ron and Hermione in the distance, jumping up and down, Ron cheering through a heavy nosebleed. (p. 225)

The first passage explains how to play Quidditch; it's informational. The second tells what happened after the game, so it's narrative. Both appear in the story along with hundreds of other pullout passages that could be labeled narrative, informational, or argument (opinion), but all serving one overriding purpose: to build the narrative.

The important thing to remember when casing a longer text to steal for a mentor passage is that writers harness the energy of different modes in service of their primary intention: to tell a story, provide information, or create an argument. To do any of these three things well means dipping into the others as the piece develops. You can tell a story to make your argument stronger; you can provide information to flesh out the setting or plotline; you can construct an argument to show different points of view by characters in a story. It's all possible.

The Story About Stories

It's interesting to note that the word *story* is used in reference to writing even when it isn't actually a narrative in the truest sense of the word. Students will write informational papers about specific topics and end them, "Thank you for reading my story." Or they'll ask, "When are our stories due?" when they're clearly writing opinion pieces. As I mentioned in Chapter 3, strong expository text feels very much like the writer is telling you a story about that topic; there's a narrative quality to writing that permeates all well-written prose. When we hear ideas expressed as stories, we tend to "get it" easier than if it's in a never-ending series of bulleted statements or lengthy paragraphs. Humans are hardwired to make meaning of life through stories, so it isn't surprising that the term is used generically sometimes to cover all writing. We learn about our past, we push forward on our present, and we dream about the future through stories.

Storyteller and researcher Kendall Haven (2007) has written a book about this very topic: *Story Proof: The Science Behind the Startling Power of Story*. He builds the case that "in our enlightened, literate, scientific, rational, advanced world, it is still story structure that lies at the core of human mental functioning." He reports,

> Results from a dozen prominent cognitive scientists and developmental psychologists have confirmed that human minds *do* rely on stories and on story architecture as the primary roadmap for understanding, making sense of, remembering, and planning our lives—as well as the countless experiences and narratives we encounter along the way. (p. vii)

It seems that as humans, we rely on story far more than we might realize.

Narrative writing is memorable and makes an impact. I'm bowled over by the number of quotes derived from narrative texts that appear on writing websites. From not only the volume but also the range of these quotes, it's clear that narrative writing seeps into every part of our reading lives. One of my favorites is from Stephen King (2002) in his book *On Writing: A Memoir of the Craft*: "Good writing…teaches the learning writer about style, graceful narration, plot development, the creation of believable characters, and truth-telling….You cannot hope to sweep someone else away by the force of your writing until it has been done to you" (p. 141). King provides us with yet one more reason to use mentor texts for narrative writing—and in truth, all forms of writing.

I have always been a big reader. But I realize now that it wasn't so much craft that I soaked up from all the reading I did before I became a professional writer. More than anything, I think reading allowed me to feel the force, the naked impact, that a great book can have on you. Reading *Bastard out of Carolina* by Dorothy Allison and *One Flew Over the Cuckoo's Nest* by Ken Kesey helped me develop a felt sense of what makes a powerful book, and how the authors were able to achieve that in these particular books.

Reading books was a crucial factor in getting me to write books for young readers. Stripped down to the bare essentials, it's a "falling in love" story. Isn't that always the way it is?

At the time, I was in a high-powered graduate writing program at Columbia University in New York City. While I was there, I started working in the city schools as a writing consultant. I'd drag a bag of picture books from class to class, reading aloud those books to students. Together, we would marvel at the lovely language, quirky characters, funny plot twists. Afterward, I'd say to students, "Think about what you just read. When you write your own story, you can do what this author did in the book we just read." I thought I was talking to the students, but I realize now that I was also talking to myself.

Falling in love is a mysterious process, and it often happens when you least expect it. One day I was reading a quiet, stunning picture book (*Owl Moon* by Jane Yolen). Suddenly I realized that it had happened: I had fallen in love with that book. In fact, I realized that I loved a number of the picture books in my bag. Those books weren't just for the students. They thrilled and enchanted and moved my soul as well.

I didn't know it at the time, but I can see now that the three inspirational taproots for my first picture book, *Twilight Comes Twice*, were *Night in the Country* by Cynthia Rylant, Marcia Brown's translation of *Shadow* by Blaise Cendrars, and *Owl Moon*. I read and reread those books so many times that I practically knew them by heart. I read them aloud, harking to the music of their sentences, watching students' reactions. After a while, I found myself saying to myself, Hmmm, I wonder if I could possibly create something like that.

I started to write. And I could "hear" those books in my mind, dimly but insistently, when I began writing *Twilight Comes Twice*. Those books set a high standard. They gave me something to shoot for, a sense of what's possible when you write a book. I'll forever be grateful to them.

Notes From Ruth

Ralph is one of my favorite writers, so I admit that I've freely stolen ideas and delicious words and phrases from his work to use with students and teachers in my own. He's a gifted wordsmith. He has the ability to capture big ideas in a simple turn of phrase. I so appreciate this glimpse into his writer's mind. I'm struck by the phrase "falling in love," because isn't that what this whole book is about? Falling in love with words, ideas, and passages from mentor texts? To understand how *Owl Moon*, for instance, got into his DNA as a reader and writer, reading it over and over, savoring the sounds of the fluency, and trying to capture the same beautiful rhythms and cadences in his own writing, is inspiring to me as both a reader and a writer.

The Traits and Narrative Writing

Getting Into the Narrative State of Mind

It's no secret to students that narrative is a powerful mode of writing. They love stories. So, here's a rich assortment of picture books that do the yeoman's work of teaching students about narrative writing, beginning with two relatively new ones that you won't want to miss because they explain how to write a story, not just be a story. Note to children's authors: We could use parallel mentor texts for informational and opinion writing, too!

Rocket Writes a Story

written and illustrated by Tad Hills
Schwartz & Wade, 2012

Rocket's literacy journey continues in this terrific sequel to *How Rocket Learned to Read*. You can teach the narrative writing process from this text, including how to find a topic, how it's organized, how to connect with the audience, how to discover the best words, and how to put them into sentences. I especially appreciate the role of the teacher in this story to inspire and nudge.

After reading and discussing *Rocket Writes a Story*, there are many possible avenues for writing. For example, I noticed that the tree of words has no verbs. It would be fun for students to go back through the text and pull out the verbs to create a new word tree. Or, maybe it would be interesting for students to consider this story from the owl's point of view. Regardless of what you and your students decide, this book is bound to inspire new writing.

. . . .

Little Red Writing

written by Joan Holub, illustrated by Melissa Sweet
Chronicle, 2013

Ms. 2, the story's pencil teacher, helps students write their own version of Little Red Riding Hood. Filled with energy and exuberance, and told through the point of view of the other pencils in the class, students will enjoy this narrative romp that reveals how to write right along with being a mentor text for the traits of writing.

Students may wish to create their own adjective path, conjunction glue, adverb motto, or pencil rules like those found on different pages of the book. It's a dizzying collection of writing possibilities—and an enchanting picture book.

The Ideas Trait and Narrative Writing

> **Ideas:** The piece's content—its central message and details that support that message

For students who cry, "I don't know what to write about," mentor texts provide much-needed relief. The main idea and how it's developed in a narrative mentor text can produce an aha moment of understanding for young writers while providing the courage to try something similar in a piece of their own. Fresh, believable characters that grow and learn, a rich setting that's easy to visualize, and events that are logically sequenced through powerful, original story lines can be demonstrated in narrative models. We look especially closely at the ideas trait to see how the writer tells a new story or puts an original twist on a familiar one. We expect the plot to be well developed and present a compelling problem that is solved—eventually.

One of the keys to success in the ideas trait is finding a new way to write about a familiar theme. It's been said that there are no new story ideas, only new takes on old ones. In my work with student writers, I find this to be a weak area, so students need lots of models and good instruction. They tend to copy another author's idea or go so far "out there" that their idea doesn't work. One of our primary jobs in teaching narrative writing is to help students see that they can take an idea from their reading that they find intriguing, and write it with a fresh perspective. And, in fact, that's not only OK but also preferred; we want to see how the mentor text launched them into fresh and original thinking of their own. Remember T.S. Eliot's line: "Mediocre writers borrow. Great writers steal." Teach your student to steal only the best and then how to create something new that's inspired by the mentor text.

Mentor Texts and the Ideas Trait

Key Quality: Finding a Topic. The writer offers a clear, central theme or a simple, original story line that is memorable.

Grandpa Green
written and illustrated by Lane Smith
Roaring Brook, 2011

Imagine being able to sculpt a garden of trees that represents a whole lifetime of memories. That's what Grandpa Green does in Lane Smith's lusciously illustrated and imaginative text. Through his artistry, he creates a memoir of his long-ago childhood, life as a soldier, and years as a husband and shows his passion for gardening.

The way Grandpa Green taps into the past by using topiary shapes is bound to give students ideas of events or people from their past, too. Help them discover that through drawing and writing, they can zero in on important topics to create memoir writing that respects and reflects their life journey so far. Have them write those ideas down and think of an artistic way to represent them in a different way than Lane Smith does with sculpture: collage, paint, crayons/markers, and other mediums.

· · · · · · · · · · · · · · · · · · · ·

Key Quality: Focusing the Topic. The writer narrows the theme or story line to create a piece that's clear, tight, and manageable.

Jangles: A Big Fish Story
written and illustrated by David Shannon
Blue Sky, 2012

"I am more than a fish. I am a storyteller, and a story," explains Jangles in this lively picture book that illustrates how to focus the topic. This book isn't about all fish or even about a type of fish; it's about one fish, Jangles, and his story. And what a fish story it is! In the fashion we've come to expect from Shannon, both the text and the pictures jump off the page and into your heart.

Help students see the benefit of focusing the topic with this text. Ask them to discuss what it's about and help them see that it's one story—only one specific and focused story, not everything in the world about fish. Then, have them take another big topic, such as sports, and do the same thing, working from the big topic to one story about sports: a time when they helped a team win a game, a time when dropping the ball contributed to losing the game, a time when they tried out a new skill with success, and so forth. Focus.

· ·

> **Key Quality: Developing the Topic.** The writer provides enough critical evidence to support the theme and shows insight on the topic, or the writer tells the story in a fresh way through an original, unpredictable plot.

"The Black Bear Story" (webpage)

written by the Black Bear Diner
(See the References section for the URL.)

I'm a big fan of going out for Sunday breakfast with friends, so imagine my delight when I looked down at the paper menu at this restaurant and found the Black Bear Diner's story. Yes, as you've already guessed, I stole it. But, in my defense, it's consumable, so it's not really a bad thing. The menu chronicles the history of the diner and the key people who opened what is now a very successful restaurant chain. The text develops as a nonfiction narrative. Everyday texts are found in the most surprising places sometimes.

Students might enjoy interviewing local businesspeople to discover the story behind their enterprises. A little legwork would have to be done to find willing store owners, but perhaps they'd be persuaded to do a phone or in-person interview if they could tell their stories—which are always fascinating. Help students plan a list of possible questions that will help them gather the details and information needed to develop their narratives. When students write up their stories, have them use the

Black Bear Diner's story as a model, and then share the results with the businesspeople who participated. Who knows? Maybe a local newspaper might be interested in picking up the stories and publishing them!

. . . .

> **Key Quality: Using Details.** The writer offers credible, accurate details that create pictures in the reader's mind, from the beginning of the piece to the end. Those details provide the reader with evidence of the writer's knowledge about and/or experience with the topic.

Inside Out & Back Again
written by Thanhha Lai
Harper, 2011

I've read this beautifully written book three times, and in each reading, I admire the writing even more. In the story, Hà, the 10-year-old protagonist, and her family flee from Saigon right as it falls from U.S. occupation, and they find themselves on a boat, heading to the United States. Written in free verse, this text is lyrical and flows across the page (you can dip into this text for the sentence fluency trait, too); it tells a powerful story, using poetic details that take your breath away.

Here are Hà's descriptions of her classmates as she begins to assimilate into her new life in Alabama:

> Fire hair on skin dotted with spots.
> Fuzzy dark hair on skin shiny as lacquer.
> Hair the colour of root on milky skin.
> Lots of braids on mild chocolate.
> White hair on a pink boy.
> Honey hair with orange ribbons on see-through skin.
> Hair with barrettes in all colours on bronze bread.
>
> I'm the only
> straight black hair
> on olive skin. (p. 142)

The text in this touching book is highly visual. The details help readers see what Hà sees—that no one looks like her, and certainly no one speaks like her either. It's a powerful and illuminating story.

Try comparing this description and the use of details with Sandra Cisneros's bilingual picture book *Hairs/Pelitos*, which was adapted from her longer powerhouse work *The House on Mango Street*. The authors of these books will help teach your students the value of writing details that paint pictures in the reader's mind.

The Organization Trait and Narrative Writing

Organization: The internal structure of the piece

Here's a real fork in the road: The organization of narrative writing looks a lot different than informational writing. Narrative, whether fiction or nonfiction, uses a chronological sequence of events. The lead can be daring and even bolder than it's informational counterpart, and the ending is often unexpected or symbolic. Time and place work in harmony in narrative writing, moving the story along seamlessly through the story line.

A key to success in narrative writing for the organization trait is pacing. Pacing is how the writer slows up events to give the reader a deeper look at what's happening, and then speeds through parts that don't need the same close inspection. It's tricky, and student writers often spend way too much time on the introduction, rush through the body, and then tack on an ending, almost as an afterthought. When done well, pacing guides the reader to and through the most significant events by using sequencing and transition words that are natural and feel effortless.

Mentor Texts and the Organization Trait

Key Quality: *Creating the Lead.* The writer grabs the reader's attention from the start and leads him or her into the piece naturally. The writer entices the reader, providing a tantalizing glimpse of what's to come.

Tuck Everlasting

written by Natalie Babbitt
Farrar, Straus and Giroux, 1975

In all of my reading years, I can't remember a lead as powerful as the one in *Tuck Everlasting*. So, although I'm recommending newer books and everyday texts throughout this book, I'm reaching back to a favorite for a mentor text in this key quality. This is one of those books that I hope will always be a part of students' reading lives. It's a classic and has cast its spell over readers for almost 40 years. You'll be able to find passages for every key quality of every trait in this flawlessly written text.

The lead in the Prologue of this book sets the stage for all the magic that's to come, and establishes the tone for the book as well.

> The first week of August hangs at the very top of summer, the top of the live-long year, like the highest seat of a Ferris wheel when it pauses in its turning. The weeks that come before are only a climb from balmy spring, and those that follow a drop to the chill of autumn, but the first week of August is motionless, and hot. It is curiously silent, too, with blank white dawns and glaring noons, and sunsets smeared with too much color. Often at night there is lightning, but it quivers all alone. There is no thunder, no relieving rain. There are strange and breathless days, the dog days, when people are led to do things they are sure to be sorry for after. (p. 3)

I'm simply spellbound by this passage and the writing skill it took to create it. Project this passage and ask students to share their reactions. Then, go through it line by line to pull out the sensory images and see how many there are, and how smoothly and elegantly they're woven into this powerful lead. Ask students how the sensory images enhance the introduction. Then, ask them to revise generic leads, such as, "Once upon a time," or "I'm going to tell you a story about…," to be more like Babbitt's.

Key Quality: Using Sequence and Transition Words. The writer includes a variety of carefully selected sequence words (e.g., *later, then, meanwhile*) and transition words (e.g., *however, also, clearly*), which are placed wisely to guide the reader through the piece by showing how ideas progress, relate, and/or diverge.

Over and Under the Snow

written by Kate Messner, illustrated by Christopher Silas Neal
Chronicle, 2011

This book is ready-made for demonstrating the pivotal role of sequence and transition words in narrative writing. It's about a day in the snow: a fun-filled, adventure-ridden, satisfyingly exhausting day. Almost every paragraph begins with the words *over* or *under*, which makes it sound like it would be terribly repetitive, but in Messner's skilled hands, it's poetic.

Point out the artful use of sequence and transition words to students as you read, and note how they're used to show location and direction. Next, brainstorm a list of additional sequence words that they could pair together, such as *up* and *out, down* and *through,* and *in* and *across* (all prepositions, by the way—a great time to explain their use in the context of writing). A quick consult with Google will provide lengthy lists if you wish to provide that as a resource. Then, ask small groups of students to pick a pair of words and work out a short story that uses them as Messner has done in her story.

. . . .

Alex the Parrot: No Ordinary Bird

written by Stephanie Spinner, illustrated by Meilo So
Alfred A. Knopf, 2012

This nonfiction narrative is a picture book, but it's organized into short chapters that help the reader navigate the content easily. It's simple to find the different informational points about Alex, the parrot, and the research about his surprising intelligence in this true story.

I found Alex's story absolutely fascinating, and I was quite surprised by how much I learned about parrots from this picture book. I also had additional questions, such as, Do all African gray parrots have this level of intelligence? What other animals are today's scientists studying for intelligence? I bet students will have questions, too, so to follow up on this book, I'd ask them to write out what they'd like to know more about and plan where that information would be inserted into the text to develop the body of the book even further. Then, compare how the body of nonfiction narrative is organized as opposed to the body of fiction narrative and note the differences and similarities in this trait.

. . . .

"The Lion King" and "The Lion King: Alternate Ending" (wiki posts)

written and hosted by Disney Studios
(See the References section for the URLs.)

The story line of the beloved movie and musical *The Lion King* is familiar to adults and children alike. But who knew that the moviemakers had tried out different endings during the script-writing process until the final one was chosen?

In the two articles that you can locate on the Disney webpages, readers find out that in the first idea for the ending, there was to have been a vicious battle between Simba and Scar that ended with Scar burning in a horrible death. In contrast, in the revised ending that was actually filmed, we understand that Scar is killed by the hyenas, but it's not graphically depicted. The film ends on a high note with the Pride Lands green and lush again and Simba and Nala's newborn cub, Kiara, continuing the circle of life. Students will want to discuss the pros and cons of both endings and why one was preferred over the other for the film. If any students have seen the musical version, ask them to recall the ending and how it compares with the film version's. Then, ask students to pick another famous story, examine the ending, and write an alternative.

The Voice Trait and Narrative Writing

Voice: The tone and tenor of the piece

The narrative or storyteller's voice is the one that most people recognize the easiest. It's often described with emotion-driven words, such as *sad, scary, thoughtful, hilarious, worried,* and *joyous.* Terms such as *compelling, expressive,* and *honest* should match the writer's use of voice overall. The writing should have energy and passion. Voice is the writer's DNA. This trait recognizes the importance of individuality. It's the writer's unique way of looking at the world and interpreting it. Voice connects the reader and writer; it's what makes you, the reader, feel so much in the moment that you can't bear to stop reading. A great story line is a key reason to continue, but voice is what keeps readers interested and reading with rapt attention.

The key to teaching students to write well with voice is to ensure that they're writing about something they care about and that they feel free to express themselves using distinctive words and phrases. We recognize the unique voices of Dr. Seuss, Mo Willems, and Dav Pilkey, for instance. By the time we've worked with student writers for a few months, we're able to hear their writing voices, too.

Mentor Texts and the Voice Trait

Key Quality: Establishing a Tone. The writer cares about the topic, and it shows. The writing is expressive and compelling. The reader feels the writer's conviction, authority, and integrity.

"Some Dude's Fry Sauce" (product description)
written by Some Dude's Fry Sauce
(See the Appendix for the reproducible.)

The story of how this fry sauce came into being is hysterically funny. It certainly got my attention as a consumer. The tone was just right to make me take a second look at the product and then put it in my shopping cart. Using a "country song"–sounding twang and playfulness with grammar, the ad writer gives us an enjoyable example of narrative writing in the everyday world.

Imagine the energy and delight of your students if they select a product to bring to class to use to write narrative ad copy using a voice that they think will get shoppers' attention. Encourage students to try different voices until they hit the tone that's right for their product. Then, send the new ad copy to the company and see what happens. Who knows? Maybe students will get a thank-you in the form of a supply of something delicious—maybe green beans!

. . . .

Key Quality: Conveying the Purpose. The writer makes clear his or her reason for creating the piece. The writer offers a point of view that's appropriate for the mode (narrative, informational, or argument), which compels the reader to read on.

chapter **CB** book

Marshfield Dreams: When I Was a Kid
written by Ralph Fletcher
Henry Holt, 2005

In an alternatingly funny, sweet, and touching series of vignettes about his childhood, Fletcher delivers the right voice for each moment in his stories. This memoir is a series of grandly told tales—family lore—that add up to a lovely tribute to the Fletcher family. From his point of view as an adult, Fletcher provides an insider's view of just what that life was like way back when. (Sorry, Ralph, but you're younger than me, if that's any consolation.) When you read the book to the end, you'll savor the last lines:

> "Coming!" I yelled back. I sat up and brushed off the pine needles. Bits of light danced in the deep forest shadows around me. I knew I'd never forget that place. Then I stood up and stepped into my new life, whatever that might be. (p. 183)

It's the perfect chord to end the perfect book for introducing memoir writing to students.

Pick a few favorite passages from the book (I love the tackle box story and the funeral scene) and share them with students to show the different ways that Fletcher conveys the purpose for each to the reader. Then, ask them to pick two or three events from their own lives that they could talk about that are a mix of purposes: a time when they learned something, a time when something hilarious happened, a time when they might have been disappointed, and so on. Have students tell their stories using a voice that conveys that purpose for writing to a partner and then make sure the partner has a turn, too.

. . . .

> **Key Quality: *Creating a Connection to the Audience.*** The writer speaks in a way that makes the reader want to listen. The writer has considered what readers need to know and the best way to convey it by sharing his or her fascination, feelings, and opinions about the topic.

Creepy Carrots!
written by Aaron Reynolds, illustrated by Peter Brown
Simon & Schuster Books for Young Readers, 2012

Who hasn't feared something creepy under the bed or in the closet in the dead of night? Reynolds taps into that universal feeling with his delightfully imaginative story about the creepy carrots that Jasper Rabbit is sure are following him around. Think of Edgar Allan Poe's voice as inspiration for the voice in this new children's story—only with a much lighter touch.

There are lines in this book that are too good to pass up for a little more attention as you read aloud. Have your students act out what the "soft…sinister…tunktunktunk of carrots creeping" sounds and feels like. Then, have them try acting out the phrase "Breathing. Terrible, carroty breathing" and see what happens. As you engage them with this original story and point out the great word choice, ask students to tell you where they felt the strongest connection to the author's voice, and then explain what it is the author did to make that work.

. . . .

Dragons Love Tacos

written by Adam Rubin, illustrated by Daniel Salmieri

Dial Books for Young Readers, 2012

What would you put on the must-have list if you were hosting a party for dragons? This original and charming story asks that question and ponders what dragons might like most about a party. It's risky because, of course, we don't actually throw parties for dragons, but students will hear the joy in this story and enjoy the surprises as they turn the pages. It's not predictable, that much I can assure you.

Daring to try something different and grow and stretch as a writer are important qualities to encourage in young students. Being right and safe isn't always the best way to go in writing, as *Dragons Love Tacos* certainly models beautifully. Ask students where the surprises are in this book—the places where the writer took a risk. Then, have students find passages that show risk in other classroom books. They might even enjoy writing to the authors with their comments about what they admire about the voice in the texts that they like best.

The Word Choice Trait and Narrative Writing

Word choice: The vocabulary the writer uses to convey meaning and enlighten the reader

Narrative writers pay special attention to the energy and liveliness of their words. They use figurative language and reach and stretch for new words, and sometimes when the right word doesn't come to mind, they make it up. The words in narrative writing need to sparkle and show pizzazz right along with being specific and correct. Writers have a little more creative leverage in narrative writing with the word choice trait than in other forms of writing where word choice focuses a great deal on precision and power.

The key to using words in narrative writing is capturing the reader's imagination by using words to bring the topic to life. Words are how the writer creates voice, too, so along with seeing the images in our minds, we appreciate when the writer helps us feel something and make a connection. Whether fiction or nonfiction narrative, words are the building blocks of the sentences that convey the ideas. Success hinges on having a good idea told brilliantly with great word choice.

Mentor Texts and the Word Choice Trait

> **Key Quality: Using Strong Verbs.** The writer uses many action words, giving the piece punch and pizzazz. The writer has stretched to find lively verbs that add energy to the piece.

The One and Only Ivan
written by Katherine Applegate
Harper, 2012

Ivan is a gorilla who lives in a cage in a roadside circus. He doesn't dwell much on his life before the Exit 8 Big Top Mall and Video Arcade; instead, he thinks a lot about the television shows he's seen, his art, and his friends, Stella the elephant and Bob the dog. And then Ruby comes along, and everything changes.

Word for word in the sentence, the verb carries the biggest responsibility on its back. In *The One and Only Ivan*, Applegate provides readers with examples of just how true this is. Here's a passage from the chapter "Poor Mack" (the human boss of the arcade): "Mack groans. He stumbles to his feet and hobbles off toward his office. Ruby watches him leave. I can't read her expression. Is she afraid? Relieved? Proud?" (p. 154). It took me about three seconds to find that passage, as Applegate uses strong verbs throughout. I'm sure there are hundreds of other examples in this finely crafted novel as well.

Show students this passage and any others that you find with equally strong verbs and ask them to highlight the active verbs. Then, ask students to work with a partner and rewrite one of the passages by taking out the strong verbs and replacing them with different forms of "to be," such as *is, am, are, was, were, be, being,* and *been.* Discuss the differences between the original text and the new version to discover which they prefer and why. Remind students that revising for verbs can be a powerful way to improve their first drafts, no matter what the purpose for writing is.

. . . .

> **Key Quality: Selecting Striking Words and Phrases.** The writer uses many finely honed words and phrases. The writer's creative and effective use of literary techniques, such as alliteration, simile, and metaphor, makes the piece a pleasure to read.

The Word Collector

written and illustrated by Sonja Wimmer, translated by Jon Brokenbrow
Cuento de Luz, 2011

Filled to the brim with phrasing such as, "Wherever there was hate and violence, she sowed words of brotherhood, love and tolerance within people's hearts," this book is simply stunning in the word choice trait. The striking words and phrases fill each page, which is presented in an artistic style that I've never seen before: They snake and weave through each illustration, making this an excellent resource for discussing the presentation trait, too.

Ask students to pick one line from the book that they like the most and illustrate it in a style of their own, noting how Wimmer's work is both beautiful and imaginative as she matches up the words and the art. Then, send students on a scavenger hunt for books in the classroom library. Tell them to find a line from a different text that's an exemplar of striking words and phrases to copy and draw so they can share with the class.

. . . .

The Scarlet Stockings Spy

written by Trinka Hakes Noble, illustrated by Robert Papp
Sleeping Bear, 2004

Trinka Hakes Noble writes about events that shaped U.S. history, giving the reader an insider's perspective by revealing what life was like during long-ago times. In this case, she takes on the view of a young girl, Maddy Rose, during the Revolutionary War period of 1777. The information in this story is based on real accounts and is a model of exceptional word choice that's specific and accurate from start to finish.

Even in a short description about Maddy Rose's clothing, the words make the passage shine: "she was a Patriot rebel from head to toe in her homespun petticoats, her linsey-woolsey dress and muslin apron, her hand-me-down shoes and woven straw hat" (p. 10). Students may enjoy drawing a picture of Maddy Rose from this passage or from others that use specific and accurate words, noting that it's the careful use of language that creates the images in their minds.

. . . .

"Cloudy With a Chance of Meatballs 2 (2013)"
(movie review)

written by Rotten Tomatoes
(See the References section for the URL.)

This lively review of an even livelier movie packs a punch in the word choice trait. Because they're usually short, reviews can be challenging writing formats. They need to pack a wallop in word choice in just a few sentences. You'll be dazzled by the funny, made-up terms that add pizzazz and interest to the review, such as *tacodiles, shrimpanzees,* and *apple pie-thons,* to name a few.

After sharing this review with students, ask them to add three more characters to the cast and provide descriptions of each. Encourage students to be imaginative with the words so they deepen the reader's appreciation for the role that each new character would play in the story. If they wish, ask students to cast the new characters with a famous actor or actress and explain their choices with words that are lively and effective.

The Sentence Fluency Trait and Narrative Writing

Sentence fluency: The way words and phrases flow through the piece

To get sentence fluency right requires multiple skills. One is fairly straightforward: writing different types of sentences. But other sentence skills are more complex and not as easy to understand: How sentences flow as they're read aloud can confound even the most seasoned writer. There's a certain "sentence sense" that writers have when they create phrasing that makes it easy on the ear. Although this is the goal for sentences in every form of writing, it's particularly true in narrative. The rhythm, the cadence, the musical quality that artfully crafted sentences have, carries the reader from one thought to the next in the progression of ideas that make up the story. Dialogue can help with fluency; it has a completely different sound than running text. And dialogue lives largely in the narrative world.

The key to sentence fluency for every purpose of writing is to read the writing aloud. No one enjoys doing this; it's a self-conscious act. Yet, the same words that seem like they're working just fine when you read them with your eyes don't always sound right when you hear them. The fix is often simple: Move a word here, a phrase there, cut parts out, add something in, move something around. (Thank goodness for word processing, where these acts are achieved without undue recopying.) The result of this revision polishes the idea so it shines through in artfully crafted simple, compound, and complex sentences that glide and flow across the page.

Mentor Texts and the Sentence Fluency Trait

Key Quality: Capturing Smooth and Rhythmic Flow. The writer thinks about how the sentences sound. The writer uses phrasing that is almost musical. If the piece were read aloud, it would be easy on the ear.

"Brady Bunch TV Show Theme Song" (lyrics)
written by Frank DeVol and Sherwood Schwartz
(See the References section for the URL.)

Song lyrics make wonderful mentor texts to model smooth and rhythmic flow in the sentence fluency trait, but finding narrative lyrics is surprisingly difficult. Well, perhaps I should clarify that finding lyrics that students *should* be reading is difficult. Violence, drugs, profanity, and topics that are not suitable for young writers abound in many narrative lyrics. So, I picked this one because it's a story, it's fun, it's clean, and it's campy.

Download the song from the webpage or YouTube, play it for students, and have them sing along; most children will already know the tune because it's been popular for years and years. Then, challenge small groups of students to write a new stanza about what happens next to the Brady Bunch, after they become one family. Remind students to use the original song's smooth and rhythmic cadence so the new stanzas fit the tempo of the original. Sing the new stanzas together when they're done. You can expect the new lyrics to be creative and hilarious.

. . . .

Key Quality: Crafting Well-Built Sentences. The writer carefully and creatively constructs sentences for maximum impact. Transition words, such as *but*, *and*, and *so*, are used to join sentences and sentence parts.

Three Hens and a Peacock

written by Lester L. Laminack, illustrated by Henry Cole
Peachtree, 2011

From the first few lines of this amusing and award-winning text, readers are drawn into the story by the lyrical way it's told. Lester Laminack writes stylishly and fluently throughout, using his artfully crafted sentences to nudge the reader into and through each hilarious event. Readers will find many creative constructions right along with traditional sentence structures as they examine the book more closely for well-built sentence models.

Project pages of the book for students and ask them to identify the different types of sentences on the page: simple, compound, and complex. If any of the constructions stump them, explain that along with the workhorse sentences, authors usually include some fragments or dialogue to break up the flow and make it sound easy on the ear. Ask students to write a short extension to the story about what happens at the end (is that an ostrich falling off the truck?) and challenge them to use well-built sentences and include dialogue, too.

. . . .

Wonder

written by R.J. Palacio
Alfred A. Knopf, 2012

Like most readers, I fell in love with this book the minute I met August Pullman. Auggie was born with a terribly deformed face, and even after many, many surgeries, it remains contorted and misshapen. When we enter Auggie's life, he's about to enter middle school, and for the first time, he'll be around groups of kids his age. His parents are worried, Auggie is worried, and school officials are worried about how to protect Auggie from stares and unkind comments. This powerful story of self-reliance and resilience is an important one for all students to know and take to heart. As I began to look at it through the eyes of the writing thief, I saw traits on every page. I was especially taken with the variety of the sentences and how they're constructed. Throughout the book, the use of dialogue adds fluency by creating a natural rhythm and flow. For example,

> I'm not saying they were doing any of these things in a mean way, by the way: not once did any kid laugh or make noises or do anything like that. They were just being normal dumb kids. I know that. I kind of wanted to tell them that. Like, it's okay, I know I'm weird-looking, take a look, I don't bite. Hey, the truth is, if a Wookiee started going to the school all of a sudden, I'd be curious, I'd probably stare a bit! (p. 62)

The use of internal dialogue makes it possible for the author to write sentences the way Auggie is thinking them. It creates interesting-sounding and natural fluency.

Ask students to try writing this passage from the point of view of one of the students who run into Auggie for the first time. Have them write what the student might have been thinking—respectfully and thoughtfully, but honestly. Let them play with sentence patterns to create a different character's internal dialogue.

· ·

> **Key Quality: Breaking the "Rules" to Create Fluency.** The writer diverges from Standard English to create interest and impact. For example, the writer may use a sentence fragment, such as "All alone in the forest," or a single word, such as "Bam!" to accent a particular moment or action. The writer might begin with informal words, such as *well*, *and*, or *but*, to create a conversational tone, or break rules intentionally to make dialogue sound authentic.

Mirror Mirror: A Book of Reversible Verse
written by Marilyn Singer, illustrated by Josée Masse
Dutton Children's, 2010

I first stole the idea for reversible writing from the YouTube video "Lost Generation." If you haven't seen it, check it out. It's based on the essay by Jonathan Reed for an AARP writing contest. When I tried to replicate the format, however, I found it really hard to get a good result: You read the piece down the page and then back up to get two completely different takes on the topic. To make this work, the author has to pay very close attention to the fluency, where the lines break, where the capitalization and punctuation go to make the phrasing smooth in either direction. Happily, I discovered Singer's picture book of reversible fairy tales that provides page after page of models for students to understand this technique. Here's an example that I wrote of what Singer calls reverso, or reading up and down the lines (only changes in punctuation and capitalization are allowed):

A cat	Incomplete:
without	A chair
a chair:	without
Incomplete.	a cat.

Because this isn't the easiest thing to do, model this writing activity for students first by picking another tale and then writing it out in reversible form. Use one of the passages in *Mirror Mirror* as a starting place. Point out how the lines break and how punctuation is used to make the text flow. Work through the process line by line, discussing the options and where the lines need to begin and end for the reversible format to work. Then, for students who are intrigued by this technique, turn them loose to try one on their own.

The Conventions Trait and Narrative Writing

Conventions: The mechanical correctness of the piece

Conventions are conventions. We use them consistently across the modes (purposes) of writing, including narrative writing. We look for grade-level control as we examine text for correct spelling, skillful use of punctuation and paragraphing, accurate capitalization, and control over Standard English grammar. There are a few differences worth noting, however, that are mostly related to narrative writing. For example, dialogue is often part of narrative writing and can present specific capitalization and punctuation challenges. In addition, I've run across writers who've experimented with creating voice by trying a dialect (remember Some Dude's Fry Sauce?).

The key to conventions in the narrative mode is that writers take liberties with Standard English to create a more authentic story and characters. Students should feel free to go outside of the conventions box now and then and use conventions for emphasis, to add voice, to develop characters, and to add to the reader's enjoyment of their pieces. This means, of course, that they're already in control of the standard conventions and *choose* to break the rules to add style, as opposed to using conventions carelessly and without concern for the reader's ability to understand the text.

Mentor Texts and the Conventions Trait

Key Quality: Checking Spelling. The writer spells sight words, high-frequency words, and less familiar words correctly. When the writer spells less familiar words incorrectly, those words are phonetically correct. Overall, the piece reveals control in spelling.

Pancho Rabbit and the Coyote: A Migrant's Tale
written and illustrated by Duncan Tonatiuh
Abrams Books for Young Readers, 2013

I really appreciate how authors take time to show readers how cultures connect. With a liberal dose of Spanish words mixed into this text, students see how Spanish is spelled alongside the excellent use of English words throughout. Because it's a folktale, sharing this book provides an opportunity to discuss the genre of folktales within the narrative mode.

When you finish sharing this well-written tale, discuss it and then go back in to pull out the Spanish words. Help students pronounce and spell them. Have students pick words from the story in English and, using a translator app or online program, translate it into Spanish or any other language that they wish to try. Make a list of the words in English, Spanish, and other languages, being careful to spell each word correctly as it's added.

. . . .

Exclamation Mark

written by Amy Krouse Rosenthal, illustrated by Tom Lichtenheld
Scholastic, 2013

I've been waiting and waiting to share this title. It's a clever and original idea—something I've come to expect from this author/illustrator team. The exclamation mark is the main character, and through the simple pictures and text, the reader comes to appreciate the story of his self-discovery. Joined by support characters, the question mark and the period, we explore the importance of finding your "inner exclamation mark" through the ingenious design and wordplay.

Share this book, savor every page, and then encourage students to write their own version from the point of view of the period or the question mark. Both have distinctive voices in this book, so the new versions should be enjoyable for students to try on their own. This activity will definitely provide a showcase for their punctuation skills.

· · · · · · · · · · · · · · · · · · ·

"10 Accidental Inventions You Won't Believe" (blog post)

written by Marianne English
(See the References section for the URL.)

Number 9 in this blog post tells the story of how corn flakes were accidentally invented by Will Keith Kellogg—a last name that students might recognize. It's a fascinating nonfiction account that's bound to intrigue you and your students. You'll likely want to read about the other accidental inventions in this blog as well. In the passage, you'll find examples of capitalization of proper nouns, cities, titles, beginnings of sentences (of course!), and the product itself.

I'm a big fan of this website, How Stuff Works. It often uses narratives to present information, which makes it all that much more interesting to read. Students may want to surf through other articles and find examples of capitalization handled correctly after you review the rules that your students know and should use every time they write.

· · · · · · · · · · · · · · · · · · · ·

> **Key Quality: Applying Grammar and Usage.** The writer forms grammatically correct phrases and sentences. The writer shows care in applying the rules of Standard English but may break those rules for stylistic reasons.

Pirates vs. Cowboys

written by Aaron Reynolds, illustrated by David Barneda
Alfred A. Knopf, 2013

Pirates and cowboys don't speak the same language, as you'll find out in this hilarious story. Who knew the trouble that would cause when Burnt Beard the Pirate and his crew head into Old Cheyenne looking for a place to bury their treasure? Reynolds plays with grammar to create both pirate- and cowboy-speak, and the result is enjoyable for all. Fair warning, however: There are guns and swords in this story, but they're used in a historical and appropriate context.

Ask students why authors, who are in full command of Standard English, might break the rules in their writing. Discuss the role of grammar in the development of a character. Then, ask students to go back with you through the text to find different grammatical constructions that Reynolds played with and decide if that was a risk worth taking, as they compare his text to the Standard English construction. Ask students to write at least one more line of dialogue that fits what the pirates and cowboys might say, and insert it in a logical place in the text.

The Presentation Trait and Narrative Writing

Presentation: The physical appearance of the piece

What works in the narrative mode for the presentation trait is the same in other modes. Here we look at the visual appeal of the sentences, paragraphs, pages, and chapters as they unfold on the page. Presentation includes handwritten and word-processed text. Creative use of presentation shows up in picture books and other materials that use appearance, such as white space and text features, to draw you in and keep you reading.

The key to presentation is readability. Whoever the intended reader is, as soon as that person opens the book or clicks on the page, it should feel like the ideas are accessible and welcoming because they're easy to read. When there's too much going on (e.g., look again at *The Word Collector*), it may have a dizzying, off-putting effect for the reader. If the text has too many words on the page, it can have a similar effect as well. We all like different styles and have strong preferences for fonts and art for our own artistic reasons. Encourage students to talk about what they like and why as they develop their appreciation for the role that presentation plays for the reader so they'll take more care on their own final drafts as well.

Mentor Texts and the Presentation Trait

Key Quality: Applying Handwriting Skills. The writer uses handwriting that is clear and legible. Whether the writer prints or uses cursive, letters are uniform and slant evenly throughout the piece. The spacing between words is consistent.

Year of the Jungle:
Memories From the Home Front
written by Suzanne Collins, illustrated by James Proimos
Scholastic, 2013

Handwriting skills don't typically matter in printed, published books and materials, but in this text, the postcards that Suzy receives from her father while he's in Vietnam are written like handwriting and stand out from the rest of the text. It's actually a handwriting font, of course, but note that although it's different from the other font used for the narration, it's readable, which is an issue with some of the handwriting our students produce.

Students might enjoy looking through books in the classroom and school library to see if some (or any) have actual handwriting in them or if they all rely on a handwriting font to look like handwriting. Discuss the effect that neat handwriting has on the reader and how social media and word processing has significantly reduced the amount of handwritten text we create in today's world. If possible, ask students to interview an adult at home or in the neighborhood, or another teacher at school, to talk about how handwriting was taught and used when he or she was young versus how it's taught and used in schools and around the world today.

. . . .

Key Quality: Using Word Processing. The writer uses a font style and size that are easy to read and a good match for the piece's purpose. If the writer uses color, it enhances the piece's readability.

The Plot Chickens

written by Mary Jane Auch, illustrated by Mary Jane Auch and Herm Auch
Holiday House, 2009

Henrietta the chicken is an avid reader, but now she wants to write a story: "It must be eggshilarating," she thinks. As she writes, Henrietta walks the reader through each step of her process, making the book a minitext for teaching story writing. *The Plot Chickens* uses many different fonts, but they're all quite legible. This is a key in the presentation trait: readability. Because picture books are artworks along with the information or stories they contain, there will be variety in the choice and size of fonts in all the books in this list and in your collections, too.

Ask students to go through the book with you and make a list of the different fonts, sizes, and styles (bold, italic, underlined) they find. Then, have students find another book and do the same thing. Compare the lists and ask students which book was more visibly appealing. Have them discuss the reasons for their decisions and relate their preferences to how they can use word processing effectively in their own writing. Hint: 10 fonts is almost always too many!

. . . .

Key Quality: Using White Space. The writer frames the text with appropriately sized margins. Artful spacing between letters, words, and lines makes reading a breeze. There are no cross-outs, smudges, or tears in the paper.

 "Think" (sign)

(See the Appendix for the reproducible.)

It's happened to all of us as we write: We run out of room. We think there's enough room when we start out, but we've misjudged. This sign is a hilarious example of the need for thought in the use of margins, spacing, and white space. We need more good thinking about writing going on than about margins and spacing, but this sign is a great launching pad for a discussion about effective use of white space.

Use the word processor and create text with no white space by writing a paragraph, taking out all the spacing between words and lines and making the margins as close to the edge of the page as possible. Discuss students' reaction to the text. Then, have students help you make a chart with guidelines for white space that they can refer to as they write. Include spacing between lines (single, double), how big the top and bottom margins should be, and how to set the left and right margins. Even though creating paragraphs is a convention, you might want to include how you want students to indicate new paragraphs as they write, too, because they affect the white space as well.

. . . .

Goodnight iPad:
A Parody for the Next Generation
written by Ann Droyd (David Milgrim, pseud.)
Blue Rider, 2011

I simply couldn't resist ending this chapter on narrative writing with a parody of *Goodnight Moon* by Margaret Wise Brown, arguably the most popular and beloved picture book of all time. When I was looking at books to steal ideas for text features, *Goodnight iPad* jumped out at me. Ann Droyd has captured the original book and its timeless message in a satirical new story that parents of youngsters hooked on their iPads will certainly relate to.

Using the same text features as the original, the author and the book designer, Michael Nelson, create a new bedtime story about the magnetic hold that screens have on today's youths (and maybe some of us oldies as well). Get a copy of the original version of *Goodnight Moon* and compare it with *Goodnight iPad*, noting all the similarities and differences, too. Point out the text features to students: running narration set off in black, character dialogue, the colors of the pictures that go along with the narration, and any other features that their sharp eyes may notice. Brainstorm a list of text features found in narrative text by examining a variety of other picture books as well and encourage students to think about this key quality of the presentation trait when they're making final copies of their stories for others to read.

For a delightful video version of this new story, search for "Goodnight iPad" on YouTube.

Wrapping Up Narrative Writing

It's simply not true what many people think: that kids have narrative writing down and only need help with informational and argument (opinion) writing. Our students need superb models and teaching in all the modes of writing, not one more than the others. I deeply fear that in this standards-driven era, the joys and benefits of narrative writing and of reading fiction will be cast aside. I hope I'm wrong. I hope we keep our hearts and minds on the bigger literacy targets and realize how much today's students need all types of reading and writing to understand and prepare for life. All writing should be conceived as telling a story—what we want the readers to know, why it's important, and why they should care. And in our stories, be they narratives, informational, or argument pieces, we should be seeking truth—truth that isn't solely reliant on facts or events.

With all of this in mind, in the next chapter, let's take a closer look at opinion writing: the precursor to the argument writing that students will be asked to develop when they reach middle school or junior high. We make progress toward that goal with opinion mentor texts that show students how to support their arguments with facts and information, relying more on credible reasoning than emotion. The mentor texts in Chapter 5 and the discussion about opinion writing will give you food for thought and abundant resources to support student writers as they develop their opinion-based thinking and writing skills.

CHAPTER 5

Argument Writing

*A*hh, now we're in the thick of it. Argument writing is the core of critical thinking. It's on everyone's minds and is the subject of almost every conversation about writing instruction in the Common Core era. What is it? How do you teach it? How is it different from persuasive writing, the traditional mode we've taught and worked with over the years that's still embedded in the NAEP standards?

Here's how I reconcile this often confusing terminology: Persuasive writing's purpose is to convince the reader by constructing an argument based on opinion, personal experience, anecdotes, data, and examples. It should include counterarguments. Although persuasive writing uses evidence that supports the writer's opinion with facts and information, it can also try to convince the reader to agree with the writer's position about a topic or to take an action by playing on the reader's emotions.

Argument writing clearly lives in the same zip code as persuasive writing. Think of it as a category, genre, or specific form of persuasive writing. Academic argument writing focuses on "claims, evidence, warrants, backing, and rebuttals," according to George Hillocks, Jr. (2011, p. xvii), a noted educational researcher. It also acknowledges the opposing point of view. Argument is a very specific form of persuasive writing that draws on the critical thinking that's essential to logic, which gets at argument's core. There's little room for personal appeal in argument writing; it's an academic form of discourse. As the Common Core State Standards (NGA Center & CCSSO, 2010b) explain,

> Arguments are used for many purposes—to change the reader's point of view, to bring about some action on the reader's part, or to ask the reader to accept the writer's explanation or evaluation of a concept, issue, or problem. (p. 23)

On first blush, the Common Core's (NGA Center & CCSSO, 2010b) definition may appear redundant with the traditional purpose of persuasive writing: to construct an argument. But persuasive writing, the bigger umbrella mode, includes marketing, advertisements, and propaganda, too—not just academic writing. As presented in the Common Core, argument writing defends and argues for claims and assertions using critical thinking skills and logic through facts, data, and judgments based on evidence from primary and secondary sources. It takes a scholarly approach to the topic.

Think of the different forms of marketing and advertising that students encounter every day that are persuasive but untrue arguments: Buy this product because it tastes great; this dog food is the best for your pet; I'll make sure you don't pay more in taxes if you vote for me; visit our amusement park for the best time of your life. These assertions are not usually backed up with empirical evidence for why they're true. Propaganda falls into this area as well: ideas and information that are often biased and misleading and aim to influence someone's beliefs or actions. Marketing and propaganda, although different in their intent, are similar in that each relies on emotion and often lacks objectivity to explain the benefit and advantage of taking a specific action.

Advertising delivers through persuasion in writing, in messaging, and in its creative approach to connecting to the audience. There's no question that it's a big part of our daily lives. As we prepare students for college and career readiness, persuasive writing is an important area to continue addressing with student writers, even if it lives on the fringe of the Common Core. Student writers will need more direct and guided instruction on writing arguments, perhaps because it's not as pervasive in their everyday lives and also because they likely haven't had as much experience with argument writing compared with its informational and narrative writing counterparts.

A Developmental Stand for Arguments (Opinions)

The Common Core State Standards recognize a developmental stand in this mode as they position argument writing in two stages: First, students learn how to write strong opinion pieces in their elementary years, then they step up to academic arguments in the secondary years. The difference between what happens in grades K–5 and grades 6–12 is the quantity and quality of the information and the academic approach used to support the writer's opinion.

In grades K–5, the term *opinion* is used to describe the type of writing done to build argument skills; it's the entry level to more scholarly argument writing. Opinions should be based in fact and contain supporting evidence to back up the writer's stand. In the secondary years, students are required to make more formal arguments by defending their positions with primary and secondary sources, providing evidence-based reasons for assertions, and assimilating different points of view that lead to one defensible, credible stand: the claim.

Because this book focuses on teaching elementary-grade students, I've found a rich cache of mentor texts to share that are driven by opinions to serve as entry points for writing arguments. After all, students don't start out with the skills necessary to write solid opinion pieces. It's a gradual process. First, we help them learn to work well with informational text. I explain to students that an argument is made up of good, solid information—with an attitude. Granted, this is a bit of an oversimplification, but in truth, every argument should be grounded in facts, data, and evidence: information. Beware of student writing that begins, "I think," or, "I believe." Instead, help students gather all the information needed to have a thorough understanding of the topic, sort through it, and from there state their opinion. At this point, writers are in a position to lay out the logical thinking that supports their opinion with facts, evidence, and data. They discover any counterarguments in this process as well. You shouldn't see "I think" in a strong opinion piece; the reader's understanding should be clear by how it is presented and supported and how opposing views are refuted.

Students should expect to do opinion writing in all classes at every grade level, not just in English language arts courses where literacy analysis provides an ideal vehicle for arguments. The emphasis on content writing in the Common Core is particularly strong in the secondary grades, but I can't think of any reason why it isn't just as applicable in grades K–5 as well. Writing about content area topics and learning how to clearly state and support opinions make perfect sense in the elementary grades where the teacher often works with all disciplines throughout the day and has more scheduling flexibility to work in meaty writing tasks such as opinion writing.

Because the Common Core specifically focuses on argument, this chapter is about information, resources, and teaching ideas to help develop students' understandings of argument writing that's based on opinions and objective reasoning. But, please don't forget to include time to talk about the other sides of persuasive writing: marketing and propaganda. These are rich and engaging areas for reading and writing instruction as well, not to mention how important it is for students to recognize the writing skills for these forms of persuasive writing and how they differ from academic argument writing.

Getting Started With Argument (Opinion) Writing

Logic is a skill that many young writers lack, yet logic is the key to writing an opinion. It's absolutely necessary that the writer follow patterns of reason as the idea of the piece develops from the beginning to the end. Students struggle in this area because they lack experience in thinking clearly and logically about topics that make good opinion pieces. Students express opinions easily—as most teachers and parents are painfully aware—but they may not have enough information, credible reasons, or evidence to provide a solid case that supports their opinions. Or, they don't consider that there's another side and address it fairly in their writing. And sometimes, as they try to back up their opinions, they fall into "logic limbo," that place where good intention meets "Huh?" It just doesn't work.

Students may write, for example, that they want to stay up later than their parents allow because it's fun and they just want to postpone bedtime. This kind of thinking doesn't pass the opinion writing test. Instead, they should be challenged to discover the average bedtime for students their age by conducting a survey, to provide research from a reliable source about how many hours of sleep are recommended for a person their age, to list what they could accomplish in an extra hour or so in the evening, and even to mention the opposing arguments that they think parents would offer in reply. "Just because I want to" is not a strong opinion position.

To get past the "I think" or "I feel" emotion-driven argument, it's important to show students effective argument techniques that develop logic and those that don't. In *An Illustrated Book of Bad Arguments*, Ali Almossawi (2013) provides 19 specific examples of common pitfalls in creating effective arguments. When I first discovered this list, I thought, What a find—teachers will love this! But it's long, so if you want the complete list, you can go right to the source, which is available in its entirety, complete with examples, online (https://bookofbadarguments. com). I've included eight of my favorites with my own definitions and examples here:

1. *"Argument from consequences" (p. 14):* Taking the stand that the claim must be valid because the consequences are too dire if it isn't (e.g., "If students don't learn how to write, it will be the downfall of Western Civilization.")

2. *"Straw man" (p. 16):* Misrepresenting, misquoting, misconstruing, or oversimplifying the facts of the opposing side of an argument (e.g., "Students who don't like to write just aren't motivated.")

3. *"Appeal to irrelevant authority" (p. 18):* Referring to someone or something that is not an authority in the subject (e.g., "Even my cats agree that learning to write is important.")

4. *"Appeal to fear" (p. 26):* Imagining a scary future that would happen if a cause of action were to occur (e.g., "If you send text messages, you'll never learn how to write a sentence.")

5. *"Hasty generalization" (p. 28):* Sampling too small or too specific of a group to draw a conclusion (e.g., "Four out of six fourth graders prefer narrative writing over informational, so it is the preferred form of writing for that age.")

6. *"Appeal to ignorance" (p. 30):* Assuming something is true by not providing any evidence that it is not (e.g., "The only way to learn to write is on the computer.")

7. *"Slippery slope" (p. 42):* Discrediting a position by arguing that it will lead to a negative series of events (e.g., "If you don't learn how to write well, you will not get a good job, and if you don't have a good job, you won't have a happy life.")

8. *"Appeal to the bandwagon" (p. 44):* Arguing that because a large group of people believe something, it must be true (e.g., "Everyone knows that writing is the key to success.")

The list in its entirety could be helpful for developing reasoning skills in strong opinion pieces. It would also be completely and totally overwhelming for students to be introduced to so many potential logic problems in argument writing all at once. Pick one type of argument fallacy and focus on what it is—why it isn't an effective argument. Then, provide alternatives that are more effective. Encourage students to bring in examples from their reading, television, or other places to share as they learn to spot weak arguments.

Think of how powerful it would be to address one common argumentative pitfall each year across the grades. By the end of middle school, students would know at least eight different logic traps to avoid in their opinion and argument pieces. This selection process would make an excellent topic for a staff meeting or district curricular work in writing: Choose one from the list per grade level and discuss how you'll make each understandable for students—with lots of examples pulled from a variety of resources. Obviously, some are easier to grasp and others harder, so tackle the more straightforward and logical ones in the elementary years and leave the tricky ones for older grades...or could this be a hasty generalization?

Twelve Angry Men *and More*

Teaching how to write an opinion piece is no easy task. Seeing and hearing opinions that show both solid and flawed reasoning may be a good option to help students wrap their heads around what this mode of writing is all about. To illustrate for students what logic and reasoning look like, find a copy of the 1957 or 1997 movie *Twelve Angry Men* and select several scenes where the jurors are arguing to convict or acquit the plaintiff. The movie is a rich resource for argumentative logic; even if your students are too young or think the movie is too long or complicated to watch from beginning to end, you can focus on a few scenes and discuss the different logic techniques that students observe. You could even show the same scenes from both movies and have students argue the case that one version is more credible than the other—and why.

Another surefire way to help students express an opinion and consider the logic required to back it up is to ask them to compare a book with its movie version. Most of the time, students prefer the book because it has more detail, they're freer to create the characters and the setting in their boundless imaginations, and the story line is complete rather than abbreviated, as is often true in the movie version. Here are a few of my favorites that may work in your classroom to get the opinion ball rolling: *The Lorax* by Dr. Seuss, *Diary of a Wimpy Kid* by Jeff Kinney, *Harry Potter and the Sorcerer's Stone* by J.K. Rowling, *Fantastic Mr. Fox* by Roald Dahl, and *Where the Wild Things Are* by Maurice Sendak.

Here's how to get started:

- Put students in groups of four based on their choice of book and movie.
- Ask each group to (re)read the chosen book and (re)watch the movie. Or, if viewing at home is not a practical option, pick one book that all students can read easily, such as *The Lorax*, and that can be read and watched at school.
- Split each group into two groups: those who liked the book version best and those who preferred the movie.
- Set up a roundtable discussion to share opinions.
- Assess the success of the discussion based on how many logical and valid arguments are made that directly reference either source.
- Report back each group's total number of arguments and congratulate students on each successful argumentative point.

Carpe Diem: Seize the Day

Hop into hot topics debated at your school and take advantage of students' opinions to show them how important it is to use logic as they discuss the issue.

- Because bullying is a hot topic at almost every school, ask students to express their opinions about what the solution might be. To introduce the notion of including the opposing point of view, ask, "What's in it for the bully?"
- Are you hearing complaints about too much homework? Ask students to state and defend their opinions by giving good solid reasons for their thinking. Then, ask, "Why is homework necessary in education?"

Marinate students all day long in the logical thinking about both sides of an issue that should make up their opinion pieces. They won't master it all overnight, but each example solidifies the core concepts of argument writing and gives them much needed practice to gain skills in this important purpose for writing.

Remember that old axiom, How do you eat an elephant? One bite at a time. Teaching how to write a well-grounded argument is a process. It begins with understanding the difference between informational writing and argument (opinion) writing. Writing techniques such as how to clearly state an opinion, what supporting information looks like, how to organize the text, the appropriate voice for the piece, the language that's appropriate for the topic, and how the sentences flow are important to develop one at a time, over time.

The Secret Is in the Nudge

I'm often concerned about the motivation factor in writing. Let's face it, if students don't enjoy writing, if all the feedback they ever get is about what they're doing wrong, this could be the worst part of their day. Students who don't feel any degree of success in writing, regardless of the mode, won't write or may become behavior problems during writing time. Learning to show every student what he or she is doing right before being overly concerned with what is wrong, then nudging to make one specific change, is well received by even the most reluctant writer.

This is the best teaching tip I know: nudge. If you can figure out what a student knows, you can gently point the way to what should be learned next. Nudging is the best use of formative assessment. When you see a writer struggling with many issues in an opinion paper, or any other purpose for writing, it's tempting to weigh in with a lot of information. Don't. It can swamp the writer. Student writers I've talked to over the years have told me that when their teachers mark up their papers with all the mistakes they've made (revision and editing), it has the cumulative effect of telling them they're no good at writing and to just throw in their writing towel. When the teacher begins with something—no matter how small—that they're doing right and then zeros in on one area and coaches them by offering one idea to improve, students overwhelmingly report that they find that approach helpful. That's the main reason I'm such a strong proponent of nudges. Give student writers a chance to learn one thing well, and then tackle the next area when it's time to move on.

For argument writing, nudging might look and sound like this:

> "Rosalina, your claim, 'Animal cruelty is wrong,' is such a powerful and passionate opinion writing topic. It's a big topic with many possible directions to develop. Would you consider focusing on one smaller aspect of this topic, such as, 'Unannounced inspections for pet owners would create safer, healthier homes for pets'? Or how about, 'People convicted of animal cruelty should not be allowed to have pets'? Have you run into any information in your research on animal cruelty that you could use to focus this topic so it's manageable?"

Nudges: First, hone in on the specific topic, then help the writer gather the information necessary to support it. The rest will come later, one nudge at a time.

We must also ratchet up our expectations of what students do over the years by scaling up. That is, the opinion piece that a third grader writes should have a specific focus and supporting information, but that same opinion in fifth grade would be supported with more information and evidence that demonstrates deeper thinking. To do this, we have to sit together in teams representing each grade level and discuss expectations, share exemplar papers that demonstrate what students do at each grade level, and document the skills needed to write strong opinion pieces (or informational pieces or narratives) at each grade level.

It's absolutely essential that we build a scope and sequence of skills for writing that spirals across the grades; without it, expectations flatten out because we limit our vision to what students learn in just one year, rather than the thoughtful accumulation of knowledge that can happen over 13 years. After all, we should anticipate that our students can and will develop the writing skills over time so they can be like Dave Barry (1981): "I can win an argument on any topic, against any opponent. People know this and steer clear of me at parties. Often, as a sign of their great respect, they don't even invite me" (para.1). Because, as the character Nick Naylor, from the movie based on the book *Thank You for Smoking* by Christopher Buckley, says, "That's the beauty of argument; if you argue correctly, you're never wrong."

The more we read, the more ideas spring from the pages. While researching for a nonfiction book about how mountains form, I became fascinated with glaciers. I couldn't stop thinking about ice a mile thick and so heavy that it can creep forward, grind granite to powder, and dramatically alter landscapes. When I finished the mountain book, I began work on one about glaciers. While doing that research, I kept bumping into references to the first migrants to reach North America. Up to a point in history, humans had never been on this continent. And then one day, they arrived. Who were they? When did they get here? How? After finishing the glacier book, I wrote *Mammoth Bones and Broken Stones: The Mystery of North America's First People.* Over the course of seven years, reading begat book begat reading begat book begat reading begat book.

Reading for information does more than inform my writing. It informs me. What I read helps me decide what I think about my subject. I wrote a book about caves. Over the course of writing that cave book and two more that followed, I learned about their fragile ecosystems that are rarely seen but too often and too easily damaged or destroyed by human activity. Do you think I have an opinion about that? You bet. To write a book about honeybees and how their lives and ours are inextricably interwoven, I read 3,000 pages of text. Honeybees are in grave danger, and a lot of it is our fault. We all have opinions about just about everything. The ones that I trust most spring from a balanced diet of reading.

Sometimes my own readers form opinions based on what I write. Years ago, a little girl read my story about a turtle that was displaced by road construction. The young reader was moved by the turtle's struggles to find a new home. She decided that something should be done to protect wildlife from human encroachment. Today she's a naturalist.

In addition to informational reading, I love reading for pleasure. But even here, the writer's part of my brain is often engaged in a subtle sort of research: How did she pull that off? What a gorgeous image!

That's the best metaphor for *boy* that I've ever seen! Some authors leave such indelible impressions on me that I go back from time to time for another lesson. E.B. White heads the list. Few writers have combined a droll sense of humor and world-class imagination with such mastery of the English language. I read him for clarity. I read him for beginnings. "'Where's Papa going with that ax?'" (White, 1952, p. 1). Sigh, I'm never going to match that. I read him for logic and structure. I read him for a booster shot on how to marshal my words: Choose a suitable design and hold to it. Use the active voice.

Another way in which I learn from reading is by contrasting how other writers treat a given subject. Once at a conference, I quoted a variety of authors describing trees. I included Hemingway, A.A. Milne, Eugene Field, Ted Geisel, Barbara Kingsolver, and Harold Bell Wright. Because I was in front of teachers, I suggested that they imagine having a class with all of those writers in it at the same elementary school age. Then, I asked how those wonderfully distinct voices might have been affected if everyone were required to write to the same test instead of following their instincts based on their experiences, their passions, their own particular geniuses.

We talk about voice as if we each receive only the one that emerges as we move from squeaky childhood to melodious middle age to squeaky senior citizen. A writer's voice is more like a ventriloquist's. We develop an ensemble of characters during the course of our careers. A narrative voice may be omnipotent, but for our stars and cast members, we speak with their weaknesses, dreams, foibles, and strengths. We produce minidramas and keep changing hats as we act out all the parts. We're directors, reporters, the Wizard of Oz. We're grass harps strummed by the wind.

Distinctions can be made among poetry, fiction, and nonfiction. But their common wellspring is life itself. They are all expressions of our human experience. So, where does reading come in? Everywhere. In every imaginable way. In all the memorable books and stories. In all the memorable ways in which they were read to us as children. In how we read them now.

The Traits and Argument (Opinion) Writing

Getting Into the Opinion State of Mind

Kelly Gallagher (2011) writes,

> If I want my students to write good persuasive pieces, for example, I need to place excellent examples of real-world persuasion next to them and have them emulate them....Students write better when they are given mentor texts to help guide them. (p. 16)

Without question, students need models to understand how opinion writing looks and feels. Readers experience firsthand the power of opinion writing in Kate DiCamillo's *Because of Winn-Dixie* when Opal convinces the grocery store owner that Winn-Dixie, the stray dog she befriends in the supermarket, is really hers—and again when she talks her father into letting her keep Winn-Dixie. These two fine examples of opinion writing are woven into this classic narrative story. They should be read and discussed as mentor texts that seek to persuade by expressing an opinion. Finding shorter passages that are opinion pieces can be very eye-opening to student writers. They see firsthand evidence of how writers have one purpose in mind—to tell a story—but they can call upon other modes (informational and argument) to enrich the reader's understanding of central themes and ideas.

What follows in this section are picture books, excerpts from chapter books, and everyday texts that will help students understand how opinions show up in writing. Great writing, by the way, that you and your students will enjoy reading and discussing for the writing craft right along with the purpose. To begin, here's one by Mélanie Watt, one of my all-time favorite picture book authors. Her Scaredy Squirrel books are usually in my workshop bag because they never disappoint and because they provide inspiration for all the traits and modes.

Have I Got a Book for You!
written and illustrated by Mélanie Watt
Kids Can, 2009

Have I Got a Book for You! clearly develops an argument for buying this book. Clever and fun, students will take pleasure in reading and discussing the different techniques and arguments that Watt supplies to convince readers that this book simply must be added to their bookshelf. The salesman is so convincing that we find out he actually sold a refrigerator to a penguin, an umbrella to a fish, and a vacuum to a gopher. There appears to be no end to his persuasive talent.

Share this hilarious story and ask students to point out the different arguments that Mr. Al Foxword uses on readers to bring them to his point of view. Ask students to tell you which they found the most trustworthy and sincere. Make a list and highlight any examples, such as using questionable data, that you'd like students to understand more about and be able to use more effectively in their own opinion pieces.

Or, try this next opinion book to warm students up on this purpose for writing (Peter Brown is another favorite author-illustrator):

Mr. Tiger Goes Wild

written and illustrated by Peter Brown

Little, Brown, 2013

The jacket cover says it all: "Hello. I am Peter Brown, and it is my professional opinion that everyone should find time to go a little wild." In his captivating story, the reader discovers that Mr. Tiger is bored with being proper all the time. Proper is all well and good, but Mr. Tiger wants to loosen up and have a little fun. So he does. Not everyone agrees with Mr. Tiger's opinion about getting a little wild, though. The way Brown ends the book is an example to readers of how to resolve conflicts so everyone wins.

Share this richly illustrated text and discuss something that students get tired of doing all the time, such as making their bed every day, washing the dishes after dinner, or doing homework. Have them create a story in which they go a little wild, and include the reaction of others to this new behavior. Be sure to encourage writers to find a way to end their stories that's respectful to everyone's point of view.

The Ideas Trait and Argument (Opinion) Writing

> **Ideas:** The piece's content—its central message and details that support that message

What's the opinion of the writer? How does the reader know? What information and details are offered to support that opinion? In much the same way as the informational and narrative modes we've already explored in this book, the success of the writing lives and dies with the ideas trait. The argument the writer makes for or against the topic rests on having solid, credible information, facts, data, and examples that add up to the credibility of the writer's opinion on the topic. We shouldn't doubt that the writer knows a lot about the topic and has formed his or her opinion with thought and due consideration.

The key to success for argument writing in this trait is clarity. We want to hear all the thinking spill forth on the page so we understand what the writer thinks and feels about the idea, but we want it all to track—each precious detail, data point, quotation, and moment of insight adding up to make the strongest possible case. Look for books and materials that offer opinions, and then help students extrapolate the reasons those opinions are valid and trustworthy, noting the different logic approaches and techniques that authors use. Use mentor texts to note how the ideas, details, data, and points of view work together to make the argument clear.

Mentor Texts and the Ideas Trait

Key Quality: Finding a Topic. The writer offers a clear, central theme or a simple, original story line that is memorable.

"Steep Hill Ahead" (sign)

(See the Appendix for the reproducible.)

First, writers figure out the topic, then they take a stand by asserting their opinion about it, one way or another. This sign cautions bike riders about a road hazard. The opinion here, of course, is that riders should take every precaution to be safe. Signs like these can make great topics for opinion writing and are easy-to-locate resources: Take a picture of opinion-based roadside signs in your town or city or scour the Internet for examples.

After discussing the big idea behind this sign, ask students to write the speech that someone would deliver to the city council to convince them that this is an important road hazard sign to create and post on the public roadways. Students may have fun creating more signs that address specific road hazards, too, and provide opinions about why they're helpful to keep the public safe. Also, ask students what's missing from this sign. I noticed the rider isn't wearing a helmet. That might be another topic that students could explore to express opinions that relate to this everyday text.

· · · · · · · · · · · · · · · · · · · ·

Just Like My Papa

written by Toni Buzzeo, illustrated by Make Wohnoutka
Hyperion, 2013

Kito, a lion cub in this warm and informational story about life on the savanna, provides readers with his opinion about why he wants to be "just like my papa, the King." From how the lions around him act, sound, move, watch, listen, and hunt, Kito learns how lions behave and what makes it possible for them to survive in the wilds of Africa. He expresses his adoration of his father's prowess from page to page, creating a list of things he admires about the King while stating over and over how much he wants to be "just like my Papa."

Ask students to write their own versions of this delightful piece by picking a different animal and writing several pages of a new text that gives reasons for why a youngster, such as a giraffe, hippopotamus, or wildebeest, would want to be just like its papa. Remind them to stick with just one animal and not try to write about every animal that interests them.

· ·

George Bellows: Painter With a Punch!

written and illustrated by Robert Burleigh, paintings by
George Bellows
Abrams Books for Young Readers, 2012

When students need a model for what an opposing viewpoint looks like, this biography of artist George Bellows would be ideal to study. There are other argumentative writing benefits to be mined from the text as well, such as critical reviews of Bellows's work, which are opinion based and show the development of a strong review.

Ask students to reread the text with you and pull out examples of different points of view or opposing arguments. Then, help students frame the development of the opinion in templates such as these: "Some people think ___, but actually ___." "At first you might think ___, but after more research, you'll realize ___." "Although it's possible that ___, it's more likely that ___." "It's true that ___, but don't forget ___." Students will also enjoy reading the reviews of Bellows's work in the book, looking up his paintings online, and then writing reviews of their own.

. . . .

Key Quality: Using Details. The writer offers credible, accurate details that create pictures in the reader's mind, from the beginning of the piece to the end. Those details provide the reader with evidence of the writer's knowledge about and/or experience with the topic.

The Day the Crayons Quit

written by Drew Daywalt, illustrated by Oliver Jeffers
Philomel, 2013

Imagine that every color of crayon in the box has an opinion about why his or her color is the best. Then, imagine what the reasons could possibly be for why each color is right. That's exactly what happens in *The Day the Crayons Quit*. Each crayon's opinion is backed up with evidence found in Daywalt's text and Jeffers's drawings! From red's concern that he's wearing out because he's being used too much, or pink's issues about not being used at all, to the feud between yellow and orange about who represents the color of the sun best, this book provides opinions with lots of supporting details and information.

Ask students to find the reasons for each color's opinion by focusing on the details in the arguments and record them on a chart. Then, invite them to write a note back to Daywalt that includes the details from the book that support his decision to choose all the colors for Jeffers's drawing at the end of the text. Or, have students pick colors that aren't included in the book and create an argument to include each in a sequel text. There are many possible writing topics that could be inspired by this clever mentor text that's a good example of using details in opinion writing.

The Organization Trait and Argument (Opinion) Writing

Organization: The internal structure of the piece

Although it may be tempting to give students a script for organizing their opinion pieces, I strongly urge you against doing that. One of the hardest parts of writing opinion pieces is learning how to use logic and evidence to support your opinion, which requires hard thinking on the part of the writer. There's no script or formula for thinking clearly and writing clearly.

The structure of opinion writing is similar to structures that support how logic appears in informational writing, except that in opinion writing, an opposing point of view should be included right along with evidence and reasons that support the writer's position. The writer will want to hold back on the counterargument until a solid argument for his or her position is established. Most arguments begin with something tantalizing about the topic and build in momentum to a critical and irrefutable point that should tip the scales to the writer's side of the issue.

The key to success for organization of opinion pieces is pacing—how the information is doled out and in what doses. If the writer shoots off all the best arguments right off the bat, the reader will be underwhelmed by the end. If the writer takes too long to make key points, the reader won't buy in quickly enough. It's tricky. Pacing is a very difficult issue for writers of all ages and in all modes. The organization trait as a whole is one of the most challenging to teach and to learn. But it doesn't get easier by using formulas; they don't promote thinking. And in the end, that's what writing strong opinions is all about: logical thinking.

Mentor Texts and the Organization Trait

Key Quality: *Creating the Lead.* The writer grabs the reader's attention from the start and leads him or her into the piece naturally. The writer entices the reader, providing a tantalizing glimpse of what's to come.

The Perfect Pet
written by Margie Palatini, illustrated by Bruce Whatley
HarperCollins, 2003

"Elizabeth really, really, *really* wanted a pet. Her parents really, really, *really* did not. They gave her a plant instead," opens this delightful story that chronicles Elizabeth's many attempts to convince her parents to get her a real, living, breathing pet. When all of her options appear thwarted, she discovers a bug and maybe, just maybe, it can become the perfect pet.

The way this story begins hooks readers right off the bat. And, it does what every good introduction sets out to do: gets right into the heart of the piece without delay. But it's Elizabeth's creative arguments that stand out in this book. Students would enjoy adding more pet examples and the pros and cons of both, taking Elizabeth's view and that of the parents as well. Encourage students to begin each example with something unexpected but revealing something about what's to come in the following argument.

. . . .

That Is Not a Good Idea!

written and illustrated by Mo Willems

Balzer + Bray, 2013

Mo Willems never disappoints. In this opinion-driven piece, the duck (or is it a goose? I can't be sure) is lured into the clutches of the wolf and right into the cooking pot! Or is she? The chick, who observes the wolf's convincing ways, cautions the duck, "That is *not* a good idea!" at every turn of events. The use of the phrase "That is **NOT** a good idea!" gains emphasis through repetition: "That is REALLY **NOT** a good idea!" "That is REALLY, REALLY **NOT** a good idea!" and so on. Each time the chick speaks, the text links the ideas, one to the next. It's a clever use of a transition statement.

Because the book is a fresh take on a familiar tale, students might enjoy coming up with another supporting cast member and writing what that animal or person might say, developing it in a series of repetitive transition statements that could become part of the story as well. (Tell them to be careful not to give away the surprise ending!)

. . . .

> **Key Quality: Developing the Body.** The writer creates a piece that's easy to follow by fitting details together logically. The writer slows down to spotlight important points or events and speeds up when he or she needs to move the reader along.

"Scribble Hero" (app review)

written by Chris Morris
(See the References section for the URL.)

Within the review section of this online article about the Scribble Hero app, readers see how the review information is organized into categories: formula, imagination, tools, sidekicks, how many can play, level of challenge, quality of animation, age appropriateness, and visual appeal. The app review wraps up with an opinion about how much fun the game is. Reviews, of course, are somewhat subjective, so pointing out all the information that Morris packs into his opinion about Scribble Hero will remind students that to be credible, even personal opinions about games should be grounded in real information.

Invite students to find a game or toy from home or the classroom to review. Have them make a list of the different aspects of the game—an expanded version of the list above—to use for comment in their reviews. Encourage students to add as much real information about the game or toy as possible to make their reviews credible. If possible, send the reviews to the game makers or an online game review site so students' work receives an authentic audience.

· · · · · · · · · · · · · · · · · · · ·

Old Henry

written by Joan W. Blos, illustrated by Stephen Gammell
Mulberry, 1987

I've loved this book for years. It's a thoughtful piece about two points of view: Old Henry's and that of his neighbors. Old Henry is a character. He loves his birds and his messy yard, and he's not into mowing the grass or making repairs to his place. None of this pleases his neighbors; in fact, they get so upset at Old Henry that he gets tired of their complaining and moves away. But Old Henry finds that he misses his neighborhood and his house, so he writes to the mayor of the town to find out if there's a compromise position that might allow him to come back. The book ends with Old Henry's letter to the mayor, which is left to the reader to answer.

Students should hold discussions about both points of view reflected in the text: Old Henry's and the neighbors'. Ask students to write opinion pieces about Old Henry returning to the neighborhood, and send them to the mayor (perhaps the principal would help out by playing this role) for arbitration. Explain that the more real evidence provided to support the position, the more likely their opinion will be the one chosen by the mayor.

The Voice Trait and Argument (Opinion) Writing

Voice: The tone and tenor of the piece

When students can't bear to stop reading, or when you're reading to them and they beg you to keep going, that's voice. The writer tosses a magic blanket over the reader that draws him or her into the text so skillfully that the reader just cuddles up closer and begs for more. Who can blame readers for not wanting to break away when they're under the writer's spell? These are powerful reading moments. It's achieved through voice: conviction, authority, credibility, insight, integrity, and honesty. These are hallmarks of voice in opinion writing as well as informational writing.

The key to success in voice for opinion writing is knowing the topic well and writing with confidence, never wavering. The reader shouldn't doubt the writer's facts and information or how they're being used to make a point. Instead, the reader should feel wrapped up in the thinking as he or she weighs the logic of the argument, not simply the writer's passion about it. The writer's belief in the topic and how skillfully he or she builds the argument for or against it comes through in voice. It's the quality that makes a connection and keeps us reading with interest and respect for the writer's opinion.

Mentor Texts and the Voice Trait

Key Quality: Establishing a Tone. The writer cares about the topic, and it shows. The writing is expressive and compelling. The reader feels the writer's conviction, authority, and integrity.

I Wanna New Room

written by Karen Kaufman Orloff, illustrated by David Catrow
G.P. Putnam's Sons, 2010

The intent of Alex, the young boy who tells this story, is crystal clear from the first page: He wants his own room. He doesn't want to share a room with his little brother, Ethan, now that Baby Annie has arrived. Alex's mission is to convince his parents that moving the two boys in together is a bad idea. Told through a series of notes between Alex and his parents, this piece is lively and clever. Readers will see the point/counterpoint approach and learn how Orloff presents both sides of the argument but, ultimately, sways readers to one side in the end.

Go through the book and make a list of the tones or voice descriptors from the book: frustrated, tired, annoyed, thoughtful, kind, joyous, compassionate, and so on. Have students pick a partner and, in the tone of their choice, add two pages to the story wherever they want to position them: one from Alex and one from the person he's writing to. Have them share their pages with other groups and discuss the use of tone in their new pages.

. . . .

> **Key Quality: Conveying the Purpose.** The writer makes clear his or her reason for creating the piece. The writer offers a point of view that's appropriate for the mode (narrative, informational, or argument), which compels the reader to read on.

Hey, Little Ant

written by Phillip Hoose and Hanna Hoose, illustrated by Debbie Tilley
Tricycle, 1998

It would be hard to find a better mentor text for opinion writing that conveys the purpose of voice more clearly than what's found in this classic picture book. When a young boy decides to squish an ant, he's surprised to hear the ant speak up and plead for his life. The two characters' points of view and their reasons for having different opinions are fully explored in dialogue that alternates pages. The book ends with the decision left in the reader's hands: Should the boy squish the ant or let him go free? The reader must carefully weigh both sides and come up with a satisfactory opinion that resolves the issue.

Ask students to discuss the reasons the boy wants to squish the ant and the reasons the ant doesn't want that to happen. Then, ask for words or descriptors to describe the voice of each character, such as *sweet, dear, caring, concerned, worried, friendly,* and *responsible* for the ant, and *unimpressed, full of bravado, surprised, careless,* and *selfish* for the boy. Tell students to write an ending to the book that's true to the voice of either the boy or the ant, expressing the character's opinion. Show students the rhyme scheme of the book as well and challenge them to use it in their ending page.

. . . .

Warp Speed

written by Lisa Yee
Arthur A. Levine, 2011

One of life's hardest lessons is learning when to stand up for yourself and when to let things go. Yee provides a good example of this lesson and what it means as she reveals the father's character in Chapter 31. He tells the story of a neighborhood bully from his childhood and how he handled himself—acknowledging regrets and offering insights. Suspicious that his son, Marley, is being bullied, the father shares the story to help his son (and the reader) relate, and offers his opinion on how to manage the bullying. It's a poignant moment in the book that develops a connection between what's happening in the story and, sadly, what most young people experience at some point in their real lives as well.

Making a connection between the reader and the writer is at the heart of the voice trait. Ask students if this passage made any connections for them and invite discussion. Then, send students to the school or classroom library to find an opinion passage in another book that strives to connect the reader and the writer through the voice. Allow time to share favorites and record the discovered qualities of voice as a resource for students to consult when they're writing their own pieces.

. . . .

"Driving While Distracted" (political cartoon)

illustrated by Jeff Parker
Florida Today, 2009
(See the Appendix for the reproducible.)

Political cartoons are opinion pieces. They're a rich resource for classrooms to understand how to convey a point of view with pictures and very few words. I especially love this one on texting while driving because it captures the inherent problems with doing both at the same time. It's an example of how writers and artists take risks to make their points clear and engaging for the reader.

Allow students to take either side of this issue and prepare the case for why their opinion makes the most sense: Text while driving, or not. Encourage them to use logic with carefully chosen data, statistics, and information gathered to support their side of the argument. After creating their short opinion pieces, group students according to their stand on the issue, give them time to combine all the thinking and research on the topic, and then have them present their ideas in a panel for the rest of the class.

The Word Choice Trait and Argument (Opinion) Writing

Word choice: The vocabulary the writer uses to convey meaning and enlighten the reader

Words are the building blocks of language, regardless of the purpose for writing: informational, narrative, or opinion. The choice of the right word or phrase creates meaning, whereas the choice of the wrong word obscures it. Reading and writing are all about using words to make meaning, so this is a critical trait to explore with student writers. Without words, we can't fully express our opinions, which is the focus of this chapter. It's the precision with language—the specific word in the right place, the choice of the "just right" word over a more common one, and using figurative language to deepen thinking—that helps opinion pieces stand tall.

The key to success in this trait is to show students how to develop a fascination with words: where they come from, how they change with usage, why one word is better than another, what words make them feel, what word choice resources they have at their fingertips, and on and on. Once students begin to fall deeply into a lifelong love affair with word choice, add discussions of subtle shades of meaning—for example, why *convince* might be a better choice than *argue* and why *believe* is stronger than *feel* in their opinion writing. Writers should never feel finished with word choice. Think of your classroom as a word choice laboratory— where experiments with language succeed and fail on a daily basis as students strive for the goal of writing that has clear, precise, striking, and luscious word choice.

Mentor Texts and the Word Choice Trait

Key Quality: Using Strong Verbs. The writer uses many action words, giving the piece punch and pizzazz. The writer has stretched to find lively verbs that add energy to the piece.

"Please Do Not..." (sign)

written by the Zoological Society of San Diego, San Diego, CA
(See the Appendix for the reproducible.)

I was struck by the creative use of the verbs in this funny but also deadly serious sign about feeding the animals the first time I read it at the San Diego Zoo in 1968. I bought a copy in the gift store and have packed and moved it more times than I can count. Except for three words at the beginning and two at the end, this sign is all verbs—verbs that are precise and active and clearly communicate the message: Leave the animals alone! Talk about a great example of an opinion piece.

There's a sister sign, too, that asks zoogoers to refrain from tampering with the plants on the zoo's property. Put students in small groups of three or four and ask them to brainstorm five verbs that might be on the plant sign, such as *trample, crush, march, squash,* and *suppress.* Create the opening words of the sign, "Please Do Not," and project it on a document camera or whiteboard. Then, invite each group to add their words to the sign. If any repeat, send the group back for a substitution. Encourage students to use verbs to create a new sign with a different topic, such as, "Please Do Not Litter."

. . . .

Key Quality: Selecting Striking Words and Phrases. The writer uses many finely honed words and phrases. The writer's creative and effective use of literary techniques, such as alliteration, simile, and metaphor, makes the piece a pleasure to read.

All the Water in the World
written by George Ella Lyon, illustrated by Katherine Tillotson
Atheneum Books for Young Readers, 2011

Lyon gives us simple yet striking prose in this lyrical informational piece that takes a decided turn toward an opinion at the end. Each page has phrasing worth reading and rereading for word choice and sentence fluency techniques.

Assign students a two-page spread and ask them to highlight their favorite words and phrases and explain why they appreciate those in particular. Have students share their choices and their reasons for choosing them with the class. Save the last two pages for a discussion about whether the primary purpose of the book is informational or opinion writing. Discuss what the author did on the last two pages to take what they've learned about water in the main part of the book and shape it into an opinion at the end. Remind students that good opinion writing is informational writing with an attitude and help them understand the role of the words to make the transition from informational to opinion writing in *All the Water in the World.*

. . . .

The Promise

written by Nicola Davies, illustrated by Laura Carlin
Walker, 2013

The young girl in this story lives by stealing from others who are also poor. It's the only life she knows, and it weighs heavy on her: "My heart was as shriveled as the dead trees in the park." One night, she grabs a bag from an old woman who won't let it go until the girl promises to plant what's inside. The promise is made. As the girl begins to keep the promise, her heart is changed. She plants and plants and plants all across the world until one night, in a dark, lonely alley, another young thief takes the bag—but not before making the promise. One of the themes of this book is the argument that giving back to the earth and to others leads to a rich and fulfilling life.

Although the words are sparse in this book, not a single one is wasted. Students who think more is better will particularly benefit from the specific and accurate selection of words from beginning to end. Ask students to explain the author's opinion and how it's shown in the words of the text. Challenge students to write one sentence (however long that might be, as long as it's grammatically correct) that encapsulates that opinion. Force them to choose each word wisely and use the mentor text as a model for how to say a lot in a little.

. . . .

chapter
CB
book

Charlotte's Web

written by E.B. White, illustrated by Garth Williams
HarperCollins, 1952

Tears ran down her cheeks and she took hold of the ax and tried to pull it out of her father's hand.

"Fern," said Mr. Arable, "I know more about raising a litter of pigs than you do. A weakling makes trouble. Now run along!"

"But it's unfair," cried Fern. "The pig couldn't help being born small, could it? If *I* had been very small at birth, would you have killed *me*?"

Mr. Arable smiled. "Certainly not," he said, looking down at his daughter with love. "But this is different. A little girl is one thing, a little runty pig is another."

"I see no difference," replied Fern, still hanging on to the ax. "This is the most terrible case of injustice I ever heard of."

A queer look came over John Arable's face. He seemed almost ready to cry himself.

"All right," he said. "You go back to the house and I will bring the runt when I come in. I'll let you start it on a bottle, like a baby. Then you'll see what trouble a pig can be." (p. 3)

Notice White's wise use of language in this passage—"trouble," "injustice," "no difference," "unfair," "cry"—and how they underscore the bigger theme: A pig shall be saved. Fern's opinion of what should happen to the runt versus that of her father sets up the tension in the story right from the start. Using words with layers of meaning helps convey the message and deepen our understanding of the importance of this scene.

Ask students to discuss the two different points of view and create a list of words used in the passage that deepen meaning (see Table 3 for an example). When students finish, talk about how the choice of the words added to their understanding of what was important in the passage.

Table 3. Deep Reading for Word Choice for *Charlotte's Web*[a]

Word Choice	Mr. Arable	Fern	Deeper Meaning (Close Reading)
1	"'A weakling makes trouble.'" (p. 3)		Not only is it hard to keep the runt alive, but it also causes problems in the litter by taking too much time from the mother pig.
2		"'But it's unfair.'" (p. 3)	Just because you're smaller (or different) than others, shouldn't you be given the same opportunities to live a happy life?
3			
4			
5			

[a]White, E.B. (1952). *Charlotte's web.* New York, NY: HarperCollins.

The Sentence Fluency Trait and Argument (Opinion) Writing

Sentence fluency: The way words and phrases flow through the piece

Less is more in sentence fluency. During revision, writers learn to tighten up sentences, start sentences different ways, trim out unnecessary words, substitute an adverb for a better verb, and cut phrases that aren't pulling their weight. Artful use of sentences in argument writing can shine a spotlight on key points in the text. For instance, students can learn to put an important piece of information in a short, declarative sentence so it's not lost in the weeds of longer, more complex sentences. Show them how to play around with sentences by modeling how you revise sentences of your own. Strip away unnecessary words. Move words around. Read your writing aloud until the sentences read smoothly.

The key to sentence fluency in all prose writing is to make sure there's variety in sentence structure and length so the piece reads aloud easily. Have students chart their sentences to gather data, and discuss what was revealed. Make a grid with four columns and as many rows as there are

Table 4. Sentence Fluency Chart Model

Sentence Number	Number of Words	First Two Words	Last Word
1	6	Less is	fluency
2	31	During revision	weight
3	17	Artful use	text
4	29	For instance	sentences
5	17	Show them	own
6	4	Strip away	words
7	3	Move words	around
8	9	Read your	smoothly

sentences in the paragraph. I used my paragraph above, which has eight sentences, as an example (see Table 4).

After reviewing my first chart, I noted that I had six sentences in the paragraph and that the last four were about the same length, so I revised. It's a more fluent paragraph now, and I can confirm that at a glance by using the new chart (Table 4) of my final eight sentences.

A chart can be used to check sentences in any piece of writing, including the mentor texts in this book. The Number of Words column shows the variety of sentence lengths. The First Two Words column provides data about how the sentences begin. And the Last Word column notes the sound and rhythm created at the end of each sentence with a single-syllable or multisyllable word. Students can chart their own sentences and discuss the results with a peer. It should lead to revision of the sentences in their writing so they have different lengths, begin differently, and have the sound the writers want at the end.

Mentor Texts and the Sentence Fluency Trait

Key Quality: Capturing Smooth and Rhythmic Flow. The writer thinks about how the sentences sound. The writer uses phrasing that is almost musical. If the piece were read aloud, it would be easy on the ear.

Each Kindness
written by Jacqueline Woodson, illustrated by E.B. Lewis
Nancy Paulsen, 2012

When you read the work of an author as talented as Woodson, you probably notice that you can teach everything about writing through her prose. *Each Kindness* is an eloquent appeal to readers to consider how compassion can lead to many good things, including friendship. She shares her opinion through beautiful, flowing sentences that shepherd the reader through the text, from first page to last, with elegance and grace. Reading opinion pieces that are this well written helps writers at many levels: They see how meaty topics are expertly handled, they see how modes can mix (e.g., an opinion can be at the center of a narrative piece), and they hear and feel the power of eloquently written prose.

Try a backward exercise with students. Assign the longer sentences (seven or more words) from the book to small groups and have them rewrite each sentence in five words, no more and no less. For example, "Each little thing we do goes out, like a ripple, into the world" (p. 19), might become, "What we do affects others." Then, have students read the passage back to the class in the order of the story. They'll likely notice that the revised sentences sound humdrum and boring and that the message is not nearly as powerful. Read the original version to students again and then ask them to comment on the differences in sentence fluency between the short sentences they wrote and Woodson's. Then send them to a piece of their own writing to revise a sentence or two for fluency.

. . . .

The Elephant Road

written by Nicola Davies, illustrated by Annabel Wright
Walker, 2013

This chapter book is a cautionary story of what happens to elephant migration when centuries-old pathways are destroyed and new towns are built and inhabited by more and more people—right in the elephants' way. Whereas some of the villagers express the opinion that they want to kill the elephants because they wreak havoc on homes and buildings, others respect the elephants' right to their traditional migration patterns and fear what will happen to the species if migration is stopped. A case for both opinions is made throughout the text as Wilen, the young protagonist, struggles to find a solution that saves the elephants and his beloved village.

Here's a passage for you to read aloud in which Wilen, the young boy from whose perspective the story is told, wrestles with the opposing opinions about the elephants and the impact of a cyclone that destroyed much of the village:

> "Without the forest, who would we be?"
> "The forest gives us our soul."
> Wilen knew that Grandpa was right. He didn't like Mr. Patchap and the way he'd talked about killing elephants as if they were just pesky flies and cutting down the forest like a patch of unruly grass. But Denngu was right, too. They had to live, they had to eat and now the cyclone had made that more difficult than ever. Wilen buried his face in his hands. It was all too difficult. Why couldn't things just stay the same? (p. 77)

Discuss the construction of the sentences; students can chart it as suggested previously. Note: Sentences can begin with *but* and be grammatically correct. It wasn't always so, but it's an accepted contemporary practice. Our language changes with usage, and the way sentences are constructed has evolved over the years to keep pace. To extend this activity into opinion writing, have students write about changes to the English language and whether they think changes are good or bad.

. . . .

"Blogging Barrier #1: The Problem of Perfectionism" (blog post)

written by Juju
(See the References section for the URL.)

There is a lot of energy in this post, and a great deal of that comes from the variety of sentence types. In this blog, Juju explains why perfectionism can be a writer's worst enemy. She provides plenty of reasons for you to agree with her opinion and offers a solution to the problem, too.

Project this passage on a digital camera and have students work with a partner to discover how many sentences are simple, compound, and complex. Ask them to notice the use of punctuation and ponder whether they think it makes the sentences more interesting and adds to the voice of the piece as well. Then, ask students to draft a "Blogging Barrier #2" piece on a topic of their choice, using a variety of sentence types to express their opinions.

. . . .

Key Quality: Breaking the "Rules" to Create Fluency. The writer diverges from Standard English to create interest and impact. For example, the writer may use a sentence fragment, such as "All alone in the forest," or a single word, such as "Bam!" to accent a particular moment or action. The writer might begin with informal words, such as *well*, *and*, or *but*, to create a conversational tone, or break rules intentionally to make dialogue sound authentic.

Outfoxed

written and illustrated by Mike Twohy
Paula Wiseman, 2013

This hilarious opinion text begins with a fragment, "A dark night." Twohy breaks "rules" like this from beginning to end, as the duck slyly convinces Fox that he's not a duck at all. Rather, the duck builds the case that he's actually a dog.

Have students make a list of all the ways the duck tries to convince Fox that he's really a dog. Ask them to think of two or three additional examples of evidence that can be added into the text to further make the duck's case. Show students the sentences in the original text and point out the creative ways that they can write the sentences in their new examples. Encourage students to read their new sentences aloud to hear if they sound right or not—an essential step to check sentence fluency, especially when taking a risk with the sentences. Read the book again with the additional reasons added in at the appropriate places. If time allows, have students write out their evidence and illustrate it, then send the new pages off to Twohy in care of the publisher. Who knows? Your class might get a response from him. Imagine how motivating that would be for young writers!

The Conventions Trait
and Argument (Opinion) Writing

Conventions: The mechanical correctness of the piece

Approach this trait through this question: Where's the thinking behind the errors? By focusing on the thinking about why a specific convention was handled the way it was, the conversation between you and students about the conventions trait will deepen over time. Position comments about conventions within informational and narrative writing as well. Ask yourself, What was the writer thinking when this mistake showed up? Correcting the thinking is a lot more successful than correcting the error over the long run. Remember this saying: "Give a man a fish, and you feed him for a day. Teach a man to fish, and you feed him for a lifetime."

The key to success for conventions in opinion writing, as well as for all other forms of writing, is to notice what's going right as well as what's going wrong. Begin your conference with a young writer with what you notice that he or she is doing that works. You can even hand the writer the red pen and say, "Circle all the correctly spelled words," for instance. Even the speller who's the most challenged will find a few, which will be affirming. Then, as you look further for what the student does with spelling, punctuation, grammar and usage, punctuation, and paragraphing, notice patterns and question the thinking behind them, replacing misunderstandings with understandings that can be applied right away.

Mentor Texts and the Conventions Trait

Key Quality: Checking Spelling. The writer spells sight words, high-frequency words, and less familiar words correctly. When the writer spells less familiar words incorrectly, those words are phonetically correct. Overall, the piece reveals control in spelling.

"Can You Raed Tihs?" (passage)

author unknown

(See the Appendix for the reproducible.)

I cdnuolt blveiee taht I cluod aulaclty uesdnatnrd waht I was rdanieg. The phaonmneal pweor of the hmuan mnid. Aoccdrnig to a rscheearch at Cmabrigde Uinervtisy, it dseno't mtaetr in waht oerdr the ltteres in a wrod are, the olny iproamtnt tihng is taht the frsit and lsat ltteer be in the rghit pclae.

The rset can be a taotl mses and you can sitll raed it whotuit a pboerlm. Tihs is bcuseae the huamn mnid deos not raed ervey lteter by istlef, but the wrod as a wlohe. Azanmig huh? Yaeh and I awlyas tghuhot slpeling was ipmorantt!

This passage has been widely distributed across the Internet. A Cambridge University study reveals that we read the first and last letter of each word, not the whole word. So, it's possible to decode this crazy passage even though most of the words aren't spelled correctly. Imagine!

Project the passage and ask students to decode and read it with a partner. Discuss any difficulties that they had with reading the words and the implications of the Cambridge study on their spelling skills. What do students think about learning to spell correctly? Is it important, or is it not? Have individual students take a pro or con side of this issue and create a short opinion piece about the importance of correct spelling. They may want to do more reading about this subject to back up their positions or claims.

· · · · · · · · · · · · · · · · · · · ·

Mockingbird

written by Kathryn Erskine
Philomel, 2010

Ten-year-old Caitlin has Asperger's syndrome and struggles to understand and connect to the emotions of other children and adults. Caitlin's older brother, Devon, was killed in a school shooting, and as she and her father mourn, her questions about loss and what sadness is reveal how difficult it is for her to understand the grieving process. In Chapter 26, Caitlin tries to convince her father to finish a chest that Devon started. It's a slow sell; it's hard for Caitlin to understand that her father's way of grieving is emotion driven and that hers is closure. This book is insightful, powerful, and important.

Internal dialogue is a hallmark of this text. To understand how Caitlin views the world and makes sense of it, Erskine wisely provides the reader with what she's thinking. It's illuminating. And because there's so much internal and external dialogue by all the characters, you'll see that the words are italicized, not put in quotation marks as is more traditionally done. Ask students to express their opinions about the effectiveness of using italics over quotation marks in this text. Then, ask them to create a short dialogue for Caitlin and her father that furthers her opinion that he should finish Devon's chest. Tell students to try punctuating it traditionally, with italics, or with another form they've discovered.

. . . .

Let's Do Nothing!

written and illustrated by Tony Fucile
Candlewick, 2009

Have you ever tried to just do nothing? It can be harder than it sounds, as the two young boys in this clever story discover. Frankie and Sal have played every game, played every sport, baked every cookie, read every book—well, basically, they've done everything. What else can they do? Sal decides to do nothing. So, he uses his powers of persuasion to get Frankie to go along in lots of zany and fun ways.

Throughout, the emphasized lines are printed in big, capital letters. Because the text is relatively simple, this convention adds to the voice of the piece, clearly signaling to the reader how the lines should be read. Ask small groups of students to come up with two or three examples of what "Let's Do Something" would look like, which is how the book ends. Encourage them to use capitals to create emphasis. Then, have students add the lines that show their opinions and capitals in action. Use the document camera to project the new lines, and note the use of capitals on the pages.

. . . .

It's Hard to Be a Verb!

written by Julia Cook, illustrated by Carrie Hartman
National Center for Youth Issues, 2008

The title of this clever book is the opinion, "It's hard to be a verb." The story is a delightful romp that explores this metaphorical idea through the point of view of Louis, a very active young lad who compares himself with verbs because he's so active: "My knees start itching. My toes start twitching. My skin gets jumpy. Others get grumpy." Many of the verbs in the text itself are highlighted as the reader gets caught up in the energy of Louis's opinion about why he can't sit still or contain his arms and legs.

The focus on verbs throughout the book is an excellent way to discuss their pivotal role in writing strong sentences. Help students find all the verbs in the piece and make a list so they have it to refer to as they write. Then, ask students to consider writing an opinion sequel, such as "It's hard to be a noun," and "It's hard to be an adjective." Invite their ideas and provide time for students to try creating new opinion pieces that feature other parts of speech.

The Presentation Trait and Argument (Opinion) Writing

Presentation: The physical appearance of the piece

Regardless of the purpose for writing—informational, narrative, or argument (opinion)—the appearance of the writing matters to the reader. Picture books, of course, use both words and pictures to capture the complete idea. The visual appeal of picture books is undeniable. Everyday texts use photos and illustrations, too, so there's usually a mix of writing and image on the page, making them easy and enjoyable to read. In chapter books, the pages are laid out using a readable font and size with margins on all four sides. Sometimes pictures are added, but they're enhancements to what's on the page: charts, graphs, drawings, maps, and so forth. Great care is taken with these longer texts to make accessing the text easy on the reader as he or she reads page after page. Depending on the resources you share, the presentation of the text will vary in style.

The key to presentation is to make the writing and art as easy to read as possible. If handwriting, encourage students to be consistent with letter shapes and spacing. If word-processing, insist on a readable font and size. Show how margins and line spacing make reading a breeze. And point out that opinion writing will likely include text features such as titles, page numbers, chapter headings, sidebars, bullets, charts and graphs, maps, and illustrations, so it's important to make them clear and easy to understand.

Mentor Texts and the Presentation Trait

Key Quality: Applying Handwriting Skills. The writer uses handwriting that is clear and legible. Whether the writer prints or uses cursive, letters are uniform and slant evenly throughout the piece. The spacing between words is consistent.

"How to Tell What Someone Is Like From Their Handwriting" (wiki post)
(See the References section for the URL.)

Handwriting is as different, one person to the next, as our fingerprints. This enjoyable article seeks to convince readers that handwriting can reveal a person's personality. Although not scientific, it's a fun piece, and students may want to try out the process of matching handwriting to personality and see if they agree with the outcome.

Give students ruled paper and ask them to write their full name in cursive on one line. Stylized printing is acceptable as well. Match up the style of their writing to one of the 10 models provided in the wiki. Label the writing with the personality type. Then, have students write a paragraph below their cursive text, agreeing or disagreeing with the personality matchup and giving specific examples for their opinion.

· · · · · · · · · · · · · · · · · · · ·

Key Quality: Using Word Processing. The writer uses a font style and size that are easy to read and a good match for the piece's purpose. If the writer uses color, it enhances the piece's readability.

Hello! Hello!

written and illustrated by Matthew Cordell
Hyperion, 2012

Image that you can't get anyone to pay any attention to you because they're all watching screens: phones, e-readers, laptops, television. "Hello? Hello!" No answer. The young girl in this story tries and tries to get someone to notice her, and when no one does, she gives up and goes outside, where she discovers a leaf, a bug, flowers, and the whole wide world. She even spots a horse, drinking from a spring that calls her by name, Lydia. Lydia rides the horse and has a great outdoor adventure until her phone begins to ring. Her absence has finally been noticed, so she heads home. Once there, she turns off everyone's electronics and convinces them to join her in the big, interesting world that waits outside.

This book is written in two fonts: an older-style bitmapped font and a printing font that resembles handwriting. The first is used on the pages where Lydia is frustrated by her family's use of screens, and the second is used when she's free outside to explore the world. Ask students to discuss how the choice of font added to their understanding of the author's message. Then, ask them to pick one point of view—more time using technology or more time playing outside—and write their opinions in a long paragraph on the computer, choosing a suitable, readable font for their pieces from the fonts in the word-processing list. Ask students to add a separate statement at the end about why their choice of font works well to support their opinion.

. . . .

Key Quality: Using White Space. The writer frames the text with appropriately sized margins. Artful spacing between letters, words, and lines makes reading a breeze. There are no cross-outs, smudges, or tears in the paper.

Duck! Rabbit!

written by Amy Krouse Rosenthal, illustrated by Tom Lichtenheld
Chronicle, 2009

Understanding white space and how the eye sees what's on the page is a visual puzzle for the reader in this book. Is the illustration a duck or a rabbit? Each page builds the case for one or the other by adding the details that might sway the reader to one point of view over another. Ultimately, the reader is left with the opinion that it's all in how you look at it! Duck and rabbit.

Show students Figure 4 and, if possible, give them a copy. Ask them to work with a partner and decide which of the two images stands out more. Have students craft a paragraph explaining the reasons for their choice and challenge them to include at least one statement that acknowledges the other point of view. Share what students write with the group and discuss the role of white space in writing and in art.

Figure 4. What Do You See, Two Faces or a Vase?

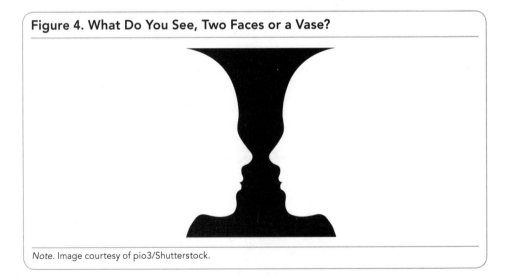

Note. Image courtesy of pio3/Shutterstock.

Duke

written by Kirby Larson
Scholastic, 2013

Chapter books have passages that can be used as exemplars of different purposes for writing other than the main purpose for the book. In this historical fiction story, Hobie Hanson decides to give up his beloved dog to the World War II fighting effort Dogs for Defense. It's a selfless act of courage. Like many brave deeds, the story has a downside: Hobie didn't realize how hard it would be to give up Duke. So, he writes a series of letters to the dog handler, expressing his opinion about why he should get his dog back. The handler writes back with news about Duke and how well he's doing but doesn't offer to send Duke home—a tough lesson for Hobie.

Duke is a chapter book that looks like most other chapter books, with all the usual text features: title page, copyright page, page numbers, chapter numbers and titles, and acknowledgments. The letters that Hobie writes to Duke's handler, Pfc. Marvin Corff, expressing Hobie's opinion that the dog should be sent home, however, are printed and set off differently from the rest of the text on the page; they're italicized and formatted to stand out. Point these letters out to students and read them a second time. Then, ask students to write a new letter from Hobie's or Pfc. Corff's point of view that could be inserted into the story using the same text features that you'd expect in a letter: greeting, body, closing, and signature.

Wrapping Up Argument (Opinion) Writing

When I began working on this chapter, I thought the hardest part would be finding enough variety in opinion mentor texts to provide a variety of resources. I was happily surprised to see how many opinion texts are available from both traditional and nontraditional sources to use as mentor texts for argument (opinion) writing. The mentor texts that I included aren't academic arguments, but the critical thinking behind each can be stolen to serve as scaffolding for what it takes to craft a logical argument or opinion. I hope you're as inspired by the mentor texts in this chapter—in all the chapters—as I am.

Do you remember that it all started with thinking about *Kinky Boots* as a model that a writing thief could use for teaching writing? Let's return to that extraordinary movie in the Epilogue to wrap up this book.

EPILOGUE

*M*onths and months have passed since I wrote the first words in this book about how the movie *Kinky Boots* can be a mentor text. Since then, I've been steeped in books, materials, and teaching ideas to add to this book. I've haunted the Internet and bookstores (all hail Amazon for two-day shipping!) and stolen liberally from many sources to find good examples of mentor texts that inspire great writing. I also went to see *Kinky Boots*, the Broadway musical. Oh, what a night.

The story line of the musical is pretty much the same as the movie version but with a few noticeable changes that incorporate the vision of Jerry Mitchell, the musical's director. I'd love to be a fly on the wall listening in on the dinner conversation between Mitchell and the movie's director, Julian Jarrold, as they discuss differences between the movie and musical story lines.

Their different artistic visions are obvious in how their respective pieces end, for instance. In the movie, Simon's father never comes to terms with who his son is and dies, estranged from Simon, now openly living as Lola. In the musical, however, the conflict is happily resolved when, at the end of his life, the father embraces Lola and expresses his love. I really love everything about Broadway musicals, but I felt like this happy ending was not authentic to the father's character, and it disconnected me from the painful truth of his voice. It reminded me, once again, of the difficulty in creating the right ending, no matter what the purpose for writing. Avid theatergoers might disagree with my assessment of the ending, but I think this is the sign of a good story—that it leaves room for discussion about the writer's and/or director's vision.

There are differences between the musical scores of the movie and musical versions, too—huge differences. In the movie, the soundtrack is made up of a series of familiar songs that add texture and energy to the production, scene by scene. In the Broadway musical, the talented Cyndi Lauper created an original musical score that's embedded into the story line rather than simply punctuating it. Both enhance the ideas, just in different ways, but I have to admit that I prefer the toe-tapping songs and especially the Milan runway music to Lauper's musical version, although I have both soundtracks on my iPod. I guess this story, no matter which form, keeps teaching me, just like *To Kill a Mockingbird* does when I reread it every summer.

In 1987, in his Academy Awards acceptance speech, Steven Spielberg said, "Only a generation of readers will spawn a generation of writers." The intertwined relationship between reading and writing could not be better expressed. Writers in today's classrooms need to be avid readers so they fully understand, from the inside out, how great writing is constructed and the impact it can have on the reader. Mentor texts, including movies, are an ideal way to show students that writing isn't simply a fixed set of skills on a linear scope-and-sequence chart, but rather a set of writing skills and thinking skills to create "mind on fire" texts of their own. Never doubt that students can learn to write, and write well, from reading.

Just think of what reading brings into a writer's life. With mentor texts and a good teacher guiding them, student writers can learn the following:

- Where ideas come from and how they play out
- How an idea develops and moves seamlessly from beginning to end
- How the writer casts a spell over the reader that lasts long after the last page is turned
- How words and phrases are used to create deep meaning and understanding
- How sentences sound and flow to serve to underscore the importance of different elements of the idea
- How conventions are used to help the reader navigate the text
- How the physical appearance of the writing is an open invitation to reading

Writing is hard. Teaching writing just may be harder. To do it well, you must approach the task from the perspective of writing as thinking. Thinking is a very challenging thing to teach, but it's ultimately satisfying when you see a student begin to problem solve, apply what has been learned, ask great questions, and get excited about how a piece of writing is turning out. This is what the National Commission on Writing for America's Families, Schools, and Colleges (2006) challenged us to embrace with its landmark report *Writing and School Reform*:

> If students are to make knowledge their own, they must struggle with the details, wrestle with the facts, and rework raw information and dimly understood concepts into language they can communicate to someone else. In short, if students are to learn, they must write. (p. 47)

This quote nails what makes teaching writing one of the toughest disciplines to master. Look at the verbs: *struggle, wrestle, rework….* These are not things kids come to easily. They're messy processes and demanding of the teacher as well as the students. They're what matter, however, if you're a writer. It's the struggle that pushes thinking about the text, and it's the reworking that brings forth the best ways to express the idea. The verbs in this quote are the key to understanding and embracing the complexities of the writing process.

Effective writing teachers don't shy away from the difficult stages of revision and editing. Instead, they use their assessment of the work to zero in on one thing at a time. Good writing teachers nudge. They ask questions like these:

- "Have you considered reworking this section to include more about what would happen if bees disappeared? Think about how Nicola Davies explained how parasites are actually essential to human health from that gross passage we read and discussed. Maybe you could make an essential connection like that with the idea in your piece right here."

- "What about breaking this paragraph apart into a bulleted list like the museum brochure we looked at today? Would that make it easier for the reader to understand your organization of the different points you're trying to make?"

- "When we read *Little Owl's Night* by Divya Srinivasan, do you remember how taken we were with the author's question, 'What happens when night turns to day?' rather than the familiar, 'What happens when day turns to night?' Could you revise this section in your piece on the water cycle with an opposite perspective that the reader won't expect for your idea and voice like Srinivasan did?"

The satisfaction with writing comes from harnessing the writing process and diving deeply into revision and editing to get it right. It isn't easy, but it's gratifying to see the writing shape up. We use mentor texts to inspire us with models and examples of what we might try in text of our own. We don't always nail it on the first try, but writing isn't diamond cutting, where there can be no allowances for mistakes. In fact, it's just the opposite; it's a recursive process built on trial and error. Each step in the direction of clarity moves us closer to good writing.

We study mentor texts to understand the moves the writer makes. I read William Zinsser's (2006) *On Writing Well: The Classic Guide to Writing Nonfiction* and realized that more is not necessarily better. That's a lesson I take away from not only what he says but also how he writes. He writes with clarity by being precise and choosing his words carefully. I read his books over and over to be reminded of the power of that important concept—something I struggle with as a writer. I read Stephen King's (2010) book *On Writing: A Memoir of the Craft* and learned that it was important to be myself on the page. My voice comes through the strongest when I stop overthinking and just write the truth as I've come to know it. I read Gary Paulsen's (1994) *Winterdance: The Fine Madness of Running the Iditarod* to encourage myself to take risks with sentences and structure. I marvel at his ability to write 48-word sentences that are grammatically correct and sing out across the page. And on and on, each author sitting by my side as I write: coaxing, nudging, teaching, questioning, urging, prodding as I struggle, just as they do, to get it down and get it right. This is a true writing workshop, where writers support and coach each other toward frissons of discovery—even when they aren't in the same room. And when I feel that frisson, I steal little bits of technique in the hopes that I can improve my writing each time. I am a writing thief, after all.

Here's a piece from children's author Lisa Yee. I saved it for the Epilogue because I think she nails the concept of reading with a writer's eye—becoming a writing thief through rereading.

The Love of Reading and Rereading

The seeds of my career began when I was very young. My mother, a first-grade teacher, read to me every night before bed. Stories like *Umbrella* by Taro Yashima, Madeline's adventures, and the tales of an elephant named Babar ushered me to sleep. When I was older, I read these stories on my own, and later many more books were added to my repertoire. But I wasn't just a reader—I was *rereader*.

I relished my weekly library visits, and when I discovered a book I loved, I'd return to it again and again. I reread works by Beverly Cleary, Mary Calhoun, and Sydney Taylor. Oh, and L. Frank Baum, Eleanor Estes, and Mary Norton. There are too many to mention them all. I knew where my favorite books resided, and after slipping a familiar title off the shelf, I'd hug it tight, as if it were an old friend. I guess it was.

Although the stories I read were vastly different, they had one thing in common: It was as if the authors were welcoming me into their families. I knew their characters intimately, and even though they were in the pages of a book, I felt like they knew me, too.

These days, I create literary families of my own. I try to populate my books with characters who seem at once new and familiar. For me, the ultimate writing test is not the Lexile level or how many books are sold, but how my words make readers feel. Have I written something someone will want to reread? I ask myself. Is this a book worth hugging?

Notes From Ruth

Lisa's books are hug-worthy, no question. They're smart, funny, wise, and insightful stories told through Lisa's original, powerful voice. When I'm in a classroom and a student has one of Lisa's books on his or her desk and comments on it, the reader/writer always grabs it, pulling it close—actually hugging it—and then says, "I love this book." Every time. It doesn't get much better than that.

Finding the books worth hugging is surely a big part of what we're trying to accomplish with readers and writers at every age. Librarians and teachers go to great lengths to provide a never-ending wellspring of powerful and transformative texts that teach students about writing, not just reading. Remember Pam Allyn's (2013) wise words: "Reading is like breathing in and writing is like breathing out" (para. 5). These great books and resources are at your fingertips, already in classrooms, schools, and public libraries and online. Double down on them and use the authors as writing mentors every day in your teaching. Breathe in and out with the writer. It'll make all the difference to you and your students. Trust me on this, fellow writing thieves.

Final Thought

Our rallying cry must be "texts not tests" as we seek to develop richer and more expansive collections of mentor texts. No one ever has enough books—even if you have bookshelves bursting at the brackets. There are always new authors to speak to students and new techniques to learn from them and try. Look at the books and materials you collect through the eyes of a writing thief. Spend your time finding new additions to your growing text collections; don't spend your time obsessing about the tests that come and go, tests that serve a role in the grand scheme of things but don't always serve students at the ground level where learning takes place every day. Texts not tests: Pass it on. It's a powerful idea whose time has come.

This book has been a joyous adventure that I realize will never end. As I look around my office, I realize that I haven't made a dent in the children's literature and everyday texts that form a huge pile around my desk, each with the potential of limitless writing inspiration hidden among the pages. I keep finding more—one of the best parts of my job! I'll always be a writing thief, pickpocketing my way through the world of print and nonprint as a writer, not just a reader. Please, come along with me. Learn to be a cat burglar of great writing and bring these priceless treasures into your teaching and learning life.

Reproducibles

"Not Just Any Gum Tree" (sign)

NOT JUST ANY GUM TREE

Koalas know that all eucalyptus is not the same.

There are nearly 900 species of eucalyptus in Australia. That would be a bountiful koala buffet except for one thing—koalas are picky eaters. And that's a good thing, because seasonal growth affects levels of toxic oils in eucalyptus leaves.

Koalas choose different species of eucalyptus depending on where they live in Australia. Without healthy forests containing a variety of different eucalyptus to choose from, koalas can run out of food, even if it looks like there are still trees around them.

Author: Zoological Society of San Diego, San Diego, CA; *Trait:* Ideas; *Key Quality:* Focusing the topic

PLEASE BE SAFE.

Do not stand, sit, climb or
lean on fences.
If you fall, animals could eat you
and that might make them sick.
Thank you.

Trait: Voice; Key Quality: Creating a connection to the audience

"Dr. Marla R. Emery, Geographer" (card)

Geography includes many different things like Geographic Information Systems (GIS) and maps. However, one important focus of geography is the relationship between people and nature – how human beings and their activities affect nature and how nature affects human beings.

Dr. Marla R. Emery
Geographer
Ph.D., Rutgers University
USDA Forest Service scientist

http://www.naturalinquirer.org   http://www.scienceinvestigator.org

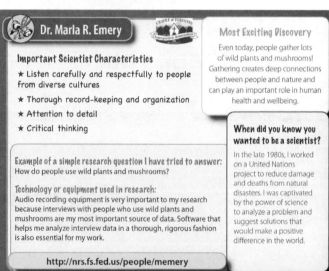

Dr. Marla R. Emery

Important Scientist Characteristics

★ Listen carefully and respectfully to people from diverse cultures

★ Thorough record-keeping and organization

★ Attention to detail

★ Critical thinking

Example of a simple research question I have tried to answer:
How do people use wild plants and mushrooms?

Technology or equipment used in research:
Audio recording equipment is very important to my research because interviews with people who use wild plants and mushrooms are my most important source of data. Software that helps me analyze interview data in a thorough, rigorous fashion is also essential for my work.

http://nrs.fs.fed.us/people/memery

Most Exciting Discovery

Even today, people gather lots of wild plants and mushrooms! Gathering creates deep connections between people and nature and can play an important role in human health and wellbeing.

When did you know you wanted to be a scientist?

In the late 1980s, I worked on a United Nations project to reduce damage and deaths from natural disasters. I was captivated by the power of science to analyze a problem and suggest solutions that would make a positive difference in the world.

Author: USDA Forest Service; *Trait:* Word choice; *Key Quality:* Using words that are specific and accurate
Visit this webpage for the card in color: www.naturalinquirer.org/scientists-v-92.html.

"Kid-Friendly Fun, Rain or Shine!" (brochure)

Author: Susquehanna River Valley Visitor's Bureau; *Trait:* Presentation; *Key Quality:* Incorporating text features
Visit this webpage for the entire brochure in color: www.the-childrens-museum.org/Kid-FriendlyActivitiesBrochure.pdf.

"Some Dude's Fry Sauce" (product description)

SOME DUDE'S FRY SAUCE

When he first mixed up a batch of "Some Dude's" fry sauce, the folks around here went crazy for it! They started puttin' it on everything from french fries, of course, to hamburgers, chicken, fish and hot dogs. Some use it as a veggie and chip dip, some have even been known to use it as shampoo (not recommended). He decided that everybody needed to have some; So, he put some of that there fry sauce in a squeezy bottle, put it in the grocery, and the rest is history.

Author: Some Dude's Fry Sauce; *Trait:* Voice; *Key Quality:* Establishing a tone

"Think" (sign)

THINK

**Do it Right
The First
Time!
Plan Ahea
d**

Trait: Presentation; *Key Quality:* Using white space

"Steep Hill Ahead" (sign)

Trait: Ideas; *Key Quality:* Finding a topic

"Driving While Distracted" (political cartoon)

Illustrator: Jeff Parker; *Trait:* Voice; *Key Quality:* Taking risks to create voice

"Please Do Not..." (sign)

PLEASE DO NOT
ANNOY, TORMENT,
PEST, PLAGUE,
MOLEST, WORRY,
BADGER, HARRY,
HARASS, HECKLE,
PERSECUTE, IRK,
BULLYRAG, VEX,
DISQUIET, GRATE,
BESET, BOTHER,
TEASE, NETTLE,
TANTALIZE, OR
RUFFLE THE ANIMALS.

The San Diego Zoo
San Diego Wild Animal Park

Author: Zoological Society of San Diego, San Diego, CA; *Trait:* Word choice; *Key Quality:* Using strong verbs

"Can You Raed Tihs?" (passage)

I cdnuolt blveiee taht I cluod aulaclty uesdnatnrd waht
I was rdanieg. The phaonmneal pweor of the hmuan
mnid. Aoccdrnig to a rscheearch at Cmabrigde
Uinervtisy, it dseno't mtaetr in waht oerdr the ltteres in
a wrod are, the olny iproamtnt tihng is taht the frsit and
lsat ltteer be in the rghit pclae.

The rset can be a taotl mses and you can sitll raed it
whotuit a pboerlm. Tihs is bcuseae the huamn mnid deos
not raed ervey lteter by istlef, but the wrod as a wlohe.
Azanmig huh? Yaeh and I awlyas tghuhot slpeling was
ipmorantt!

Author: Unknown; *Trait:* Conventions; *Key Quality:* Checking spelling

REFERENCES

Alliance for Excellent Education. (2007). *Making writing instruction a priority in America's middle and high schools.* Washington, DC: Author.

Allyn, P. (2013, July 26). Voices and choices: The secrets to summer reading and writing success [Web log post]. Retrieved from www.huffingtonpost.com/pam-allyn/voices-and-choices-the-secrets-to-summer-reading_b_3643867.html

Almossawi, A. (2013). *An illustrated book of bad arguments.* New York, NY: JasperCollins.

Barry, D. (1981). *How to argue effectively.* Retrieved from www.davebarry.com/gg/misccol.htm

Bridges, L. (2013, August 6). Rethinking the 'five finger rule.' *Scholastic Frizzle.* Retrieved from frizzleblog.scholastic.com/post/rethinking-five-finger-rule

Calkins, L.M. (1986). *The art of teaching writing.* Portsmouth, NH: Heinemann.

Coulmas, F. (1999). Writing system. In *The Blackwell encyclopedia of writing systems* (p. 560). Malden, MA: Blackwell.

Culham, R. (2003). *6 + 1 traits of writing: The complete guide, grades 3 and up.* New York, NY: Scholastic.

Culham, R. (2005). *6 + 1 traits of writing: The complete guide for the primary grades.* New York, NY: Scholastic.

Culham, R. (2010). *Traits of writing: The complete guide for middle school.* New York, NY: Scholastic.

Expository Writing Program. (n.d.). *Information about expository writing.* Retrieved from www.stanford.edu/~arnetha/expowrite/info.html

Fadiman, A. (2007). Ice cream. In *At large and at small: Familiar essays* (pp. 43–59). New York, NY: Farrar, Straus and Giroux.

Faigley, L. (1994). Competing theories of process: A critique and a proposal. In S. Perl (Ed.), *Landmark essays on writing process* (Vol. 7, pp. 149–164). Davis, CA: Hermagoras. (Reprinted from *College English*, 1986, *48*(6), 527–542)

Fletcher, R. (2011). *Mentor author, mentor texts: Short texts, craft notes, and practical classroom uses.* Portsmouth, NH: Heinemann.

Fletcher, R., & Portalupi, J. (2001). *Writing workshop: The essential guide.* Portsmouth, NH: Heinemann.

Fredricksen, J.E., Wilhelm, J.D., & Smith, M.W. (2012). *So, what's the story? Teaching narrative to understand ourselves, others, and the world.* Portsmouth, NH: Heinemann.

Gallagher, K. (2011). *Write like this: Teaching real-world writing through modeling and mentor texts.* Portland, ME: Stenhouse.

Graham, S., & Perin, D. (2007). *Writing next: Effective strategies to improve writing of adolescents in middle and high schools—A report to Carnegie Corporation of New York.* Washington, DC: Alliance for Excellent Education.

Graves, D.H. (1983). *Writing: Teachers and children at work.* Exeter, NH: Heinemann Educational.

Groll, E. (2013, July 15). Wikipedia's most interesting opening paragraph ever? *Tri-City Herald*, p. A7.

Haven, K. (2007). *Story proof: The science behind the startling power of story.* Westport, CT: Libraries Unlimited.

Hazlitt, H. (1993). *The wisdom of Henry Hazlitt* (H.F. Sennholz, Ed.). Irvington-on-Hudson, NY: Foundation for Economic Education.

Hillocks, G., Jr. (2011). *Teaching argument writing, grades 6–12: Supporting claims with relevant evidence and clear reasoning.* Portsmouth, NH: Heinemann.

King, S. (2002). *On writing: A memoir of the craft.* New York, NY: Pocket. doi:10.1215/9780822383512-002

King, S. (2010). *On writing: A memoir of the craft* (10th anniv. ed.). New York, NY: Scribner.

Krashen, S. (2011a, June 5). *Our schools are not broken: The problem is poverty.* Commencement speech presented at the Graduate School of Education and Counseling, Lewis and Clark College, Portland, OR. Retrieved from www.substancenews.net/articles.php?page=2319&section=Article

Krashen, S. (2011b). Protecting students against the effects of poverty: Libraries. *The NERA Journal, 46*(2), 17–21.

Muijs, D. (2010). Effectiveness and disadvantage in education: Can a focus on effectiveness aid equity in education? In C. Raffo, A. Dyson, H. Gunter, D. Hall, L. Jones, & A. Kalambouka (Eds.), *Education and poverty in affluent countries* (pp. 85–96). New York, NY: Routledge.

Murray, D.M. (1985). *A writer teaches writing* (2nd ed.). Boston, MA: Houghton Mifflin.

Murray, D.M. (1997). *The craft of revision* (3rd ed.). Fort Worth, TX: Harcourt Brace College.

National Center for Education Statistics. (2012). *The nation's report card: Writing 2011* (NCES 2012-470). Washington, DC: National Center for Education Statistics, Institute of Education Sciences, U.S. Department of Education.

National Commission on Writing for America's Families, Schools, and Colleges. (2006). *Writing and school reform.* New York, NY: College Board.

National Governors Association Center for Best Practices & Council of Chief State School Officers. (2010a). *Common Core State Standards for English language arts and literacy in history/social studies, science, and technical subjects.* Washington, DC: Authors.

National Governors Association Center for Best Practices & Council of Chief State School Officers. (2010b). *Common Core State Standards for English language arts and literacy in history/social studies, science, and technical subjects: Appendix A: Research supporting key elements of the standards and glossary of key terms.* Washington, DC: Authors.

Paulsen, G. (1994). *Winterdance: The fine madness of running the Iditarod.* Orlando, FL: Harcourt.

Perl, S. (Ed.). (1994). *Landmark essays on writing process* (Vol. 7). Davis, CA: Hermagoras.

Proust, M. (1993). The captive. In *In search of lost time: Vol. 5. The captive, the fugitive* (pp. 1–559; C.K.S. Moncrieff & T. Kilmartin, Trans.). New York, NY: Random House.

Ray, K.W. (1999). *Wondrous words: Writers and writing in the elementary classroom.* Urbana, IL: National Council of Teachers of English.

Ray, K.W. (with Laminack, L.L.). (2001). *The writing workshop: Working through the hard parts (and they're all hard parts)*. Urbana, IL: National Council of Teachers of English.

Ray, K.W. (2002). *What you know by heart: How to develop curriculum for your writing workshop*. Portsmouth, NH: Heinemann.

Rosenberg, A. (2006). *Madeleine L'Engle*. New York, NY: Rosen.

Sanders, W.L., & Rivers, J.C. (1996). *Cumulative and residual effects of teachers on future student academic achievement* (Research Progress Report). Knoxville, TN: University of Tennessee Value-Added Research and Assessment Center. Retrieved from www.cgp.upenn.edu/pdf/Sanders_Rivers-TVASS_teacher%20effects.pdf

Sanders, W.L., Wright, S.P., & Langevin, W.E. (2008). *Do teacher effect estimates persist when teachers move to schools with different socioeconomic environments?* (Working Paper 2008-20). Nashville, TN: National Center on Performance Incentives, Vanderbilt University's Peabody College.

Sherman, J. (2010, February 14). Consciously unconscious: Reflections on the annual social psychology conference [Web log post]. Retrieved from www.psychology today.com/blog/ambigamy/201002/consciously-unconscious-reflections-the -annual-social-psychology-conference

Sloan, R. (2012). *Mr. Penumbra's 24-hour bookstore*. New York, NY: Farrar, Straus and Giroux.

Smith, F. (1994). *Writing and the writer* (2nd ed.). Hillsdale, NJ: Erlbaum.

U.S. Department of Education, Institute of Education Sciences, National Center for Education Statistics. (2012). *Fast facts: SAT scores* (NCES 2012-001). Washington, DC: Author. Retrieved from https://nces.ed.gov/fastfacts/display.asp?id=171

U.S. Department of Education, Institute of Education Sciences, National Center for Education Statistics. (n.d.). *National Assessment of Adult Literacy (NAAL)*. Retrieved from nces.ed.gov/naal/kf_demographics.asp

U.S. Department of Education, National Institute of Literacy. (2013, April 28). *Illiteracy statistics*. Retrieved from www.statisticbrain.com/number-of-american-adults -who-cant-read/

Wright S.P., Horn, S.P., & Sanders, W.L. (1997). Teacher and classroom context effects on student achievement: Implications for teacher evaluation. *Journal of Personnel Evaluation in Education, 11*, 57–67.

Zinsser, W. (2006). *On writing well: The classic guide to writing nonfiction* (30th anniv. ed.). New York, NY: HarperCollins.

Children's Literature Cited

Allen, S., & Lindaman, J. (2006). *Written anything good lately?* Minneapolis, MN: Millbrook.

Applegate, K. (2012). *The one and only Ivan*. New York, NY: Harper.

Auch, M.J. (2009). *The plot chickens*. New York, NY: Holiday House.

Babbitt, N. (1975). *Tuck everlasting*. New York, NY: Farrar, Straus and Giroux.

Bang, M. (2012). *Ocean sunlight: How tiny plants feed the seas*. New York, NY: Blue Sky.

Barretta, G. (2007). *Dear Deer: A book of homophones*. New York, NY: Henry Holt.

Berne, J. (2008). *Manfish: A story of Jacques Cousteau*. San Francisco, CA: Chronicle.

Blos, J.W. (1987). *Old Henry*. New York, NY: Mulberry.

Brown, D. (2004). *Odd boy out: Young Albert Einstein*. Boston, MA: Houghton Mifflin.

Brown, P. (2013). *Mr. Tiger goes wild*. New York, NY: Little, Brown.

Bryant, M.E. (2010). *Oh my gods! A look-it-up guide to the gods of mythology (Mythlopedia)*. New York, NY: Scholastic.

Burleigh, R. (2012). *George Bellows: Painter with a punch!* New York, NY: Abrams Books for Young Readers.

Buzzeo, T. (2013). *Just like my papa*. New York, NY: Hyperion.

Collins, S. (2013). *Year of the jungle: Memories from the home front*. New York, NY: Scholastic.

Cook, J. (2008). *It's hard to be a verb!* Chattanooga, TN: National Center for Youth Issues.

Cordell, M. (2012). *Hello! Hello!* New York, NY: Hyperion.

Cronin, D. (2011). *M.O.M. (Mom operating manual)*. New York, NY: Atheneum Books for Young Readers.

Davies, N. (2004). *Poop: A natural history of the unmentionable*. Somerville, MA: Candlewick.

Davies, N. (2013). *The elephant road*. London, UK: Walker.

Davies, N. (2013). *The promise*. London, UK: Walker.

Daywalt, D. (2013). *The day the crayons quit*. New York, NY: Philomel.

Droyd, A. (D. Milgrim, pseud.). (2011). *Goodnight iPad: A parody for the next generation*. New York, NY: Blue Rider.

Erskine, K. (2010). *Mockingbird*. New York, NY: Philomel.

Ferris, J.C. (2012). *Noah Webster & his words*. Boston, MA: Houghton Mifflin Harcourt.

Fletcher, R. (2005). *Marshfield dreams: When I was a kid*. New York, NY: Henry Holt.

Floca, B. (2013). *Locomotive*. New York, NY: Atheneum Books for Young Readers.

Fox, K.C. (2010). *Older than the stars*. Watertown, MA: Charlesbridge.

Fucile, T. (2009). *Let's do nothing!* Somerville, MA: Candlewick.

Harrison, D.L. (2007). *Cave detectives: Unraveling the mystery of an Ice Age cave*. San Francisco, CA: Chronicle.

Hills, T. (2012). *Rocket writes a story*. New York, NY: Schwartz & Wade.

Holub, J. (2013). *Little red writing*. San Francisco, CA: Chronicle.

Hoose, P. (2012). *Moonbird: A year on the wind with the great survivor B95*. New York, NY: Farrar, Straus and Giroux.

Hoose, P., & Hoose, H. (1998). *Hey, little ant*. Berkeley, CA: Tricycle.

Huget, J.L. (2013). *The beginner's guide to running away from home*. New York, NY: Schwartz & Wade.

Lai, T. (2011). *Inside out & back again*. New York, NY: Harper.

Laminack, L.L. (2011). *Three hens and a peacock*. Atlanta, GA: Peachtree.

Larson, K. (2013). *Duke*. New York, NY: Scholastic.

Lyon, G.E. (2011). *All the water in the world*. New York, NY: Atheneum Books for Young Readers.

McReynolds, L. (2012). *Eight days gone*. Watertown, MA: Charlesbridge.

Messner, K. (2011). *Over and under the snow*. San Francisco, CA: Chronicle.

Moss, M. (2006). *Dr. Amelia's boredom survival guide: First aid for rainy days, boring errands, waiting rooms, whatever!* New York, NY: Simon & Schuster Books for Young Readers.

Noble, T.H. (2004). *The scarlet stockings spy.* Chelsea, MI: Sleeping Bear.

Orloff, K.K. (2010). *I wanna new room.* New York, NY: G.P. Putnam's Sons.

Palacio, R.J. (2012). *Wonder.* New York, NY: Alfred A. Knopf.

Palatini, M. (2003). *The perfect pet.* New York, NY: HarperCollins.

Perdomo, W. (2010). *Clemente!* New York, NY: Henry Holt.Reynolds, A. (2012). *Creepy carrots!* New York, NY: Simon & Schuster Books for Young Readers.

Reynolds, A. (2013). *Pirates vs. cowboys.* New York, NY: Alfred A. Knopf.

Rosenthal, A.K. (2009). *Duck! Rabbit!* San Francisco, CA: Chronicle.

Rosenthal, A.K. (2013). *Exclamation mark.* New York, NY: Scholastic.

Rowling, J.K. (1999). *Harry Potter and the sorcerer's stone.* New York, NY: Scholastic.

Rubin, A. (2012). *Dragons love tacos.* New York, NY: Dial Books for Young Readers.

Schaefer, L.M. (2013). *Lifetime: The amazing numbers in animal lives.* San Francisco, CA: Chronicle.

Shannon, D. (2012). *Jangles: A big fish story.* New York, NY: Blue Sky.

Shannon, D. (2013). *Bugs in my hair!* New York, NY: Blue Sky.

Singer, M. (2010). *Mirror mirror: A book of reversible verse.* New York, NY: Dutton Children's.

Smith, L. (2011). *Grandpa Green.* New York, NY: Roaring Brook.

Spinner, S. (2012). *Alex the parrot: No ordinary bird.* New York, NY: Alfred A. Knopf.

Thimmesh, C. (2000). *Girls think of everything: Stories of ingenious inventions by women.* Boston, MA: Houghton Mifflin.

Thimmesh, C. (2006). *Team Moon: How 400,000 people landed* Apollo 11 *on the moon.* New York, NY: Houghton Mifflin.

Tonatiuh, D. (2013). *Pancho Rabbit and the coyote: A migrant's tale.* New York, NY: Abrams Books for Young Readers.

Truss, L. (2006). *Eats, shoots and leaves: Why, commas really do make a difference!* New York, NY: G.P. Putnam's Sons.

Twohy, M. (2013). *Outfoxed.* New York, NY: Paula Wiseman.

Watt, M. (2009). *Have I got a book for you!* Tonawanda, NY: Kids Can.

White, E.B. (1952). *Charlotte's web.* New York, NY: HarperCollins.

Willems, M. (2013). *That is* not *a* good *idea!* New York, NY: Balzer + Bray.

Wimmer, S. (2011). *The word collector* (J. Brokenbrow, Trans.). Madrid, Spain: Cuento de Luz.

Woodson, J. (2012). *Each kindness.* New York, NY: Nancy Paulsen.

Yee, L. (2011). *Warp speed.* New York, NY: Arthur A. Levine.

Everyday Texts

Black Bear Diner. (2014). *The Black Bear story.* Retrieved from blackbeardiner.com/about-us/

DeVol, F., & Schwartz, S. (1969). *Brady Bunch TV show theme song* [Lyrics]. Retrieved from kids.niehs.nih.gov/games/songs/favorites/bradymp3.htm

Disney Studios. (n.d.). *The Lion King.* Retrieved from disney.wikia.com/wiki/The_Lion_King

Disney Studios. (n.d.). *The Lion King: Alternate ending.* Retrieved from disney.wikia.com/wiki/The_Lion_King:_Alternate_Ending

English, M. (2013, October 22). 10 accidental inventions you won't believe: Corn flakes (#9) [Web log post]. Retrieved from www.geniusstuff.com/blog/list/10-accidental -inventions/

Hasbro. (n.d.). Angry Birds Go! Jenga Pirate Pig Attack Game [Product description]. Retrieved from www.hasbro.com/shop/details.cfm?R=51293D04-5056-9047-F556 -9050B953517A:en_US

How to tell what someone is like from their handwriting. (n.d.). [Web log post]. Retrieved from www.wikihow.com/Tell-What-Someone-is-Like-from-Their -Handwriting

Juju. (2013, May 9). Blogging barrier #1: The problem of perfectionism [Web log post]. Retrieved from kidbloggersclub.com/blogging-barrier-1-problem-of -perfectionism/

Morris, C. (2013, August 28). *Here, kitty kitty: Monopoly rolls out its new token.* Retrieved from games.yahoo.com/blogs/plugged-in/kitty-kitty-monopoly-rolls -token-180239913.html

Morris, C. (n.d.). Scribble Hero [App review]. Retrieved from www.commonsense media.org/mobile-app-reviews/scribble-hero

O'Neil, L. (2013, June 28). School kids correct celebrity grammar mistakes on Twitter [Web log post]. Retrieved from www.cbc.ca/newsblogs/yourcommunity/2013/06/ school-kids-correct-celebrity-grammar-mistakes-on-twitter.html

Parker, J. (2009, October 2). *Driving while distracted* [Political cartoon]. *Florida Today.* Retrieved from www.floridatoday.com/content/blogs/jparker/2009/10/1002 -cartoon-driving-while-distracted.shtml

Rotten Tomatoes. (2013). Cloudy with a chance of meatballs 2 (2013) [Movie review]. Retrieved from www.rottentomatoes.com/m/cloudy_with_a_chance_of _meatballs_2_2013/

INDEX

Note. Page numbers followed by *f* or *t* indicate figures or tables, respectively.

fonts: handwriting, 43, 124; legibility of, 125; style and size of, 43, 86; using different, 171

foreign languages, 121

formative assessment, 136

4Ws of writing: fitting together of, 30; overview of, 21–22; writing modes, 22, 25–26, 30, 50; writing process, 22–23, 30, 34–37, 35; writing workshop, 22, 25, 30, 178. *See also* writing traits

Fox, K.C., 73

Fox, M., 8

Frankel, T., 46*f*

Fredricksen, J.E., 26

Fucile, T., 168

Gallagher, K., 140

Gammell, S., 150

generalizations, in argument (opinion) writing, 133

genres, nonfiction, 54

Graham, S., 10, 31

grammar, 43, 83–84; in argument (opinion) writing, 169; contemporary practices for, 162–163; in narrative writing, 123; playful use of, 108–109

Graves, D.H., 22

Groll, E., 55

handwriting: in argument (opinion) writing, 170; fonts that look like, 43, 124; in informational writing, 85; in narrative writing, 124–125

Harrison, D.L., 78, 138–140

Hartman, C., 169

Hasbro, 79

hasty generalization arguments, 133

Haven, K., 95

Hazlitt, H., 72

headings, 87, 173

heterogeneity of classrooms, 20

Hillocks, G., Jr., 26, 129

Hills, T., 98

Holub, J., 98

homophones, 81–82

Hoose, H., 152

Hoose, P., 61–62, 152

Horn, S.P., 20

how-to format, 69

Huget, J.L., 69

ideas: being a thief of, 6; definitions/descriptions of, 24, 57, 99, 142; development of, 40; in informational writing, 54

ideas trait and argument (opinion) writing: developing topics, 144–145; finding and developing a topic, 143; focusing the topic, 144; overview, 142–143; using details, 145–146

ideas trait and informational writing: developing the topic, 61–62; finding a topic, 59; focusing the topic, 60; mentor texts for getting started, 58–63; overview, 57–58; using details, 62

ideas trait and narrative writing: developing the topic, 101–102; finding a topic, 99–103; focusing the topic, 100–101; overview, 99; using details, 102–103

ignorance, appeals to, 133

illustrated children's books, 56–57

images/imagery, 74; in all writing, 139, 140; through word choice, 114; visual narrative, 103

informal tone, 80

informational/explanatory writing mode: compared with narrative writing, 93, 94; definitions of, 26, 54; elements of, 51–54; factors in strong, 54; keys to successful, 58; models of, 87; purpose/modes for, 50; storytelling in, 90–91; studying others' writing in, 27; transitioning to opinion in, 156. *See also* ideas trait and informational writing; organization trait and informational writing; presentation trait and informational writing; sentence fluency trait and informational writing; word choice trait and informational writing

inserting capitalization: in argument (opinion) writing, 168; in informational writing, 83

internal dialogue, 118, 167

italics, 167

Jeffers, O., 145

joy of writing, 53

Juju, 163

Keats, E.J., 8

King, S., 95, 178

Kinney, J., 135

Kirsch, V.X., 64

Krashen, S., 11

Lai, T., 102–103

Laminack, L.L., 7–9, 117

Langevin, W.E., 20